No Barrier Too Great

The true story of two Romanian
Christians who triumphed over
enormous opposition and suffering

John Miles M.A. Ph.D.

& Cornel Lemnariu

O&U

Onwards & Upwards

Onwards and Upwards Publishers

4 The Old Smithy
Rockbeare
Exeter
EX5 2EA
United Kingdom
www.onwardsandupwards.org

First edition, published in the United Kingdom by Onwards and Upwards Publishers Ltd. (2019).

ISBN: 978-1-78815-555-7
Typeface: Sabon LT
Graphic design: LM Graphic Design

Endorsements

John Miles has an interesting background, giving him an insight into life in the Soviet Union. His own story, *Are We Nearly There Yet?*, is a fascinating account of journeys with his family, who started asking that question not long after starting the journey! Journeys were taking Bibles to Communist countries when it was not possible for Christians to buy them in bookshops. He has also written about the terrible events in Northern Uganda through the 'Lord's Resistance Army', *Overcoming the Powers of Hell*, and also about the Rwanda genocide of 1994, *Rwanda Rising from the Ashes*.

I commend this book about the way God worked in the life of two young Romanians who, through much suffering and pain, were married and made a new life in the UK near friends who had helped them cope with their suffering in Romania. The book shows how trust in God is rewarded in ways which are often miraculous.

The Right Reverend Kenneth Barham OBE
Former Bishop of the diocese of Cyangugu in Rwanda

Acknowledgements

This account of Cornel and Cati's remarkable lives is their own story, told to me by word of mouth or through Skype conversations. In this respect it could be considered as an autobiography. Their motive is to testify to God's love and provision in their lives. Some additional information about Romania, its economy and the politics affecting it are drawn from the Internet and from my own experiences gained from travelling to Romania many times and extensively within the country.

My thanks to Hillary Burridge for her patient help in correcting the text. Thanks also to my wife Grace for reading each chapter and then the completed text. She corrected mistakes and made useful suggestions in improving and clarifying the text. Cornel read every chapter and then the entire text, making corrections and drawing on his remarkable memory to add historically accurate details to their story, some of which relate to events from many years ago when he and Cati were children and later teenagers. Cornel's nephew Vio also related his and Ana's story in the same way, calling on their memories and verbally sharing their experiences in which they too found God to be a faithful and loving father.

Contents

No Barrier Too Great

CHAPTER ONE

Revolution

THE NOISE THAT ATTRACTED CORNEL LEMNARIU'S ATTEN-
tion at about 11:45 on the morning of 22nd December 1989 was unusual;
he looked up and saw that it was the sound of a helicopter passing low
overhead. It had taken off from a nearby rooftop and it seemed to dip
and struggle to gain height as it lost the 'push-up' effect of the flat roof
from which it was desperately escaping. The crowds of demonstrators in
Palace Square below gasped and pointed as the helicopter's powerful
twin-engines eventually gained enough lift for it to rise into the leaden
winter skies above Romania's capital city of Bucharest. Cornel observed
this from an unusual vantage point. Balancing on his crutches he was
standing on a small second floor balcony in the Foisor Orthopaedic
hospital in the centre of the city. At this moment he had no idea who was
in the helicopter or its purpose. So far, apart from the alarming sound of
gunfire, all the movement and noise had been in the streets below.

This small balcony was a touch of luxury that only this little 'private'
ward (containing just three beds) enjoyed. This ward was reserved for
patients who were considered important, such as Communist Party
members and government officials. Cornel certainly didn't belong to
these favoured elite, but he had befriended someone who did occupy one
of the beds in this special ward and they often visited each other to talk
and try to while away the boredom of the hours, days and weeks during
their stay in this hospital. Such favouring of the country's elite was
normal, not just in Romania, but throughout most of the communist
world – 'those who were more equal than the others'! In a country that
had very little food for sale to ordinary citizens, good food and even
luxury goods could be purchased from the 'dollar shops' with hard
currency such as American dollars or German deutschmarks.

Cornel was often in this hospital; in fact, he had spent at least a month there, and sometimes much longer, every year since the age of eighteen. He was now twenty-four years old. Most of his time in hospital had been marked by a mixture of pain, discomfort and boredom. But now, something historic was happening in the city below and although confined to a hospital ward, Cornel was witnessing a deadly and decisive conflict being enacted before his eyes. The result of this conflict would decide the very future of his nation and its beleaguered people.

For several days, gunfire, sometimes at night with intimidating tracer rounds, had echoed around the streets and the open square adjacent to the hospital. Cornel first heard the gunfire when he was in the bathroom, but didn't know what it was since he had never heard it before. Someone in the ward, who had been in the army and knew the sound of gunfire, told him. He then began watching, from this very balcony, people shouting and running – often, literally for their lives – in the streets below.

Other patients and medical staff had warned him to stay clear of the balcony for his own safety, lest a stray bullet came his way. He ignored their caution and was not afraid; in fact, he spent many hours there trying to work out exactly what was happening. His medical condition did not allow him to sit because he could not bend at the waist or knees and the long periods of standing with the aid of his crutches was tiring. The protests that had begun in Opera Square (later renamed 'Victory Square') in the city of Timisoara in the far west of Romania on 16th December had come to Bucharest's Palace Square (later renamed Revolution Square); to the heart of the repressive regime of Nicolae Ceauşescu and to most of the larger cities in Romania. The Romanian revolution of December 1989 had reached its dramatic climax!

The word 'revolution' is historically used most often in reference to the communist revolution that first began with the Russian revolution in 1917, which eventually spread – mostly by violence and intimidation – to many other countries during the Twentieth Century. At its height it encompassed almost half the world's population. In Romania the word is still used frequently – but since December 1989, with a very different, even opposite, meaning. Every year on 22nd December, Romania celebrates the end of the brutal and corrupt communist dictatorship that had blighted their country for forty-two years. In the jargon of the communist vocabulary, it would probably be described as a 'counter-revolution'. For the Romanian people, this was their own revolution. It was a people's revolution, achieved through demonstrations, courage and bloodshed, fuelled by a deep anger.

Russia had experienced a radical change of direction when Nikolai Gorbachev became General Secretary of the Communist Party of the Soviet Union in March 1985, which led eventually to the break-up of the Soviet Union. The key change which he announced was that Russia would no longer interfere in the affairs of their neighbours. This was a financial necessity as well as a political change. Keeping military control over the Warsaw Pact block and supporting places such as Cuba, Mozambique and Angola was costing more than the almost-bankrupt Russian economy could stand. Soon all the countries under Soviet domination took the hint and declared independence from Soviet control, and communism collapsed in these countries. Romania, which was never a very enthusiastic member of the Warsaw Pact, was the penultimate 'domino' to fall. This left just Albania where communism was ousted by an election in March 1992.

As the helicopter growled its way towards the horizon, word quickly spread around the hospital that it was the President's personal helicopter and it was being shown on television. Patients and staff rushed to the female ward which had the hospital's only television. This was a small ward and about thirty people were crushed in there watching the television screen in amazement. Cornel left the balcony and squashed in with the others to watch a scene so momentous that at first it was difficult to take it all in. The crowds of demonstrators and the departure of the President's helicopter lifting off from the roof had all been filmed and was now being replayed on national television just minutes after the events had actually happened. The government's agents moved quickly to try to shut it all down, but it was too late. Everyone now knew that the President Nicolae Ceauşescu was in that helicopter. Only later were the events of that morning pieced together, and to this day some of the facts are confusing and events disputed. What cannot be doubted was that Ceauşescu's thirty-two-year communist dictatorship was finally over!

The generally accepted order of events on this historic day are as follows. At 11:20 a.m. on 22nd December 1989, Ceauşescu's personal helicopter pilot, Lt. Col. Vasile Maluţan, received urgent instructions from Lt. General Traian Opruta to proceed to Palace Square quickly to pick up the President. Col. Maluţan and his co-pilot, who were well aware of the rising tension in the city, were on permanent standby and they were soon airborne. This open square sat in front of the Central Committee Headquarters of the Romanian Communist Party and was the obvious place to pick up anyone from that building. The base for the helicopter was only a few minutes' flight from Palace Square, so the helicopter soon arrived overhead. As Col. Maluțan hovered over Palace Square he saw it was impossible to land there because it was filled with thousands of angry demonstrators. As he circled the building wondering what he should do, he saw a man brandishing a white net curtain from one of the windows waving him down to land on the flat terrace roof on one side of this large building. The white Dauphin 203 Helicopter landed on the spacious rooftop terrace at 11:44 a.m.

Nicolae Ceaușescu and his wife Elena had left it very late to make their escape from the growing crowds of demonstrators who were at that very moment storming the Central Committee Headquarters. As late as 10.00 a.m. that morning, Ceaușescu had chaired his last meeting inside the Central Committee building, announcing that he had taken over the leadership of the army due to the 'extremely serious situation'. He also informed them that he had declared a state of emergency throughout the country. Such was his delusional state of mind, he thought that he could still retain control of the country.

The day before, he had attempted to make a speech from the balcony overlooking Palace Square. Government supporters and reluctant busloads of people from the villages near the capital were brought in to form a cheering crowd – except there wasn't much cheering! Earlier that day, Ceaușescu had told the Defence Minister Vasile Milea (a three-star General and Romania's most senior army officer) to order the army to fire on the crowds of demonstrators. He refused and was immediately sacked for treason. Gen. Milea was already in disfavour with Ceaușescu for sending troops to quell the uprising in Timisoara without live ammunition. His body was found later in his office, but the news had already spread through senior army staff that Ceaușescu had ordered him to be shot. The army believed that Gen. Milea had been executed. This caused the rank-and-file soldiers and their officers to largely switch sides to the revolution. The military commanders made no effort to keep their men loyal to the government. The death of Gen. Milea was undoubtedly a major factor in turning the army against Ceaușescu that day, and eventually led to his own death. Some sources said that the General had tried to wound himself to escape his position and had mistakenly bled to death. Not many people believe this unlikely tale.

The crowd swelled as tens of thousands of workers from the big industrial sites, waving Romanian flags with the central communist emblem cut out, were headed towards Palace Square and the nearby University Square, where the previous day the security forces resorted to shooting protesters to clear the square. By now the sympathies of the police and their militia had turned in favour of the protestors. The demonstrators now easily outnumbered the Party faithful who had obediently formed up in front of the building. They began to boo, throw stones and chant, "Tim-is-oara, Tim-is-oara," in protest at those who had been shot and the many that had died in Opera Square, Timisoara, the city where the revolution had begun. In what has become the iconic footage of the Romanian revolution, filmed and broadcast around the world, Ceaușescu, not long into his speech with its usual rhetoric, stumbled as a look of fear came over his face. His guards hustled him and his wife off the balcony and into the building.

As the crowd broke through the heavy doors of the building, Ceaușescu and his wife Elena, with four senior aides, were heading for the roof in an elevator to reach the helicopter that had just landed. Then, adding to the panic of those making their escape, the elevator broke down! The doors had to be forced open by guards to allow the escapees to eventually make it to the roof. Further panic ensued when they realised that the Aérospatiale Dauphin 203 only had four passenger seats for the six people trying to board. And so, suffering a further ignominy, all six somehow squashed uncomfortably into the four seats. This meant that the helicopter was now seriously overloaded. The protesters managed to overpower Ceaușescu's bodyguards and rushed through his office and onto the balcony, then up to the roof, just as the helicopter's twelve-metre rotor blades were increasing revolutions enough to take off and gain height. The demonstrators were now invading the terrace itself but didn't risk approaching the helicopter that was obviously about to take off. There is, however, a film of demonstrators waving from the terrace to the crowds in the square below, with the helicopter beginning to take off behind them.

They landed at Snagov, about forty kilometres north-east of Bucharest where Ceaușescu had a residence. There they shed two of their passengers and took off again heading for the city of Târgoviște, eighty-two kilometres north-west of Bucharest. Col. Maluțan, who didn't like what was going on and didn't want to be involved, was ordered over the radio by the army to land his helicopter immediately. Fearing they might be shot down, he landed and the party abandoned the helicopter and then proceeded by road in a commandeered car. On the outskirts of Târgoviște they were stopped by local police who were listening to the radio, who then handed them over to the army. The army were wary of any attempt to rescue the Ceaușescus so they drove them around a large military area in an armoured personnel carrier for at least two days. The dreaded Securitate secret police force and members of the Ceaușescu family were a powerful force and could quickly mount a rescue attempt had they known the location of the Ceaușescus. There is a filmed record of them finally exiting the armoured vehicle, looking very dishevelled. The military made sure that they were filmed and that the footage was broadcast around the world. The military knew that whatever happened next had to be a *fait accompli* and needed to happen quickly.

Early on Christmas Day, 25th December 1989, in a small room in Târgoviște the Ceaușescus were tried before a court convened on orders of the National Salvation Front, Romania's quickly-formed provisional government. At the end of the short show-trial the Ceaușescus were found guilty and sentenced to death. A soldier standing guard in the proceedings was ordered to take the Ceaușescus out back, one by one and shoot them, but the Ceaușescus demanded to die together. The soldiers agreed to this and began to tie their hands behind their backs which the Ceaușescus protested against but were powerless to prevent. A firing squad of four (some accounts say three) soldiers was quickly assembled and as soon as the Ceaușescus were placed against a wall, the soldiers opened fire. Their dead bodies were filmed, and the gory images once again broadcast to the world, lest anyone might doubt that this evil couple who had terrorised and impoverished their nation were truly gone. The Ceaușescus were the last people to be executed in Romania before the abolition of capital punishment on 7th January 1990.

As Cornel Lemnaru gazed intently at the departing helicopter, and then at the now famous television images that he saw as he squeezed into the women's ward with the others, he did not yet realise that this was a revolution – and one that would eventually pave the way for an amazing revolution in his own difficult life and the personal battles he faced daily.

CHAPTER TWO

From a Village I Was Chosen

CORNEL LEMNARIU WAS BORN ON 4TH MARCH 1965, twelve days after Romania's notorious and cruel dictator Nicolae Ceaușescu became General Secretary of the Romanian Communist Party. He became Romania's second communist leader, three days after the death of his predecessor, Gheorghe Gheorghiu-Dej. Two years later he became President. Cornel's father Gheorghe Lemnariu was aged thirty-one and his mother Maria was thirty-five.

Cornel was the youngest of their seven children – five boys and two girls. They lived in the small village of Horlăceni, Botosani County, in Romania's northernmost region of Moldova, very close to the border with the Ukraine. Moldova has traditionally been the poorest of Romania's three historic regions. The other two regions are Wallachia in the south (where the capital city of Bucharest is situated) and Transylvania in the west, the largest of the three. The Romanian Orthodox Church has always been strong in Moldova and it is famous for its many monasteries built by Voivode (Ruler) Stephen III who reigned for forty-seven years from 1457 to 1504. He is usually known as 'Ştefan cel Mare', which means 'Stephen the Great'. Visiting tourists soon notice that many streets and squares are named after this Ruler, not just in Moldova, but also in other parts of Romania.

Cornel's parents were typical of Moldova's rural population who managed their peaceful lifestyle well enough without help or interference from the communist central government. They worked long days in the fields, beginning in the early spring and carrying on until late autumn.

Cornel remembers a happy childhood, and despite the poverty of the family, the seven siblings had a lot of fun together. At the time, Cornel was far too young to appreciate the difficulties that his parents were having in trying to make ends meet. They sometimes had a real struggle to find food for the day for such a large family. Cornel's mother was a very good cook and he always enjoyed what she prepared for them. As a family, they got on well together. The winter season usually meant severe weather with heavy snow and temperatures often well below freezing.

The children were responsible for looking after the animals that belonged to the family; they had two cows, some pigs, sheep and of course a lot of chickens. They had no regular source of cash income, and they had to raise the animals to provide food for themselves. Cornel went regularly with the sheep to the forest to feed them, while his older brothers would look after the cows. They sometimes went to the forest to pick mushrooms and wild strawberries, which they would either sell or use as food. Their cows provided them with milk and cheese. To create a little cash income, Cornel's mother, who was a good tailor, earned some extra money with this skill, especially in the winter months when work in the frozen fields was not possible.

In the Bleak Mid-Winter

Pavel is a Romanian evangelist who bravely ministered in the Moldovan region for many years under the communist regime. He often paid the price for preaching and was persecuted and beaten by the police. Even after the revolution it took him some years to completely lose his fear of officials in uniform. During the harsh winter months when people were unable to work the fields, they were largely confined to activities in their homes.

The rest of the year, and especially at harvest time, people were very busy in the fields; it was difficult to persuade them to attend special evangelistic meetings or even to come to church. This meant that a lot of Pavel's evangelisation needed to be conducted in the cold winter months. This led to a saying, sometimes repeated by Pavel and others, that the winter was "the springtime of the soul!"

One evening, Cornel was in the forest with all his brothers, gathering wild mushrooms. As they were about to go home with full baskets, suddenly, his brother Mircea saw a herd of wild pigs not far from them – and they were coming their way! Wild pigs really are wild and dangerous; they had no choice but to run as fast as they could. With baskets full of mushrooms which they had worked all evening to pick, they hurtled through the trees trying not to lose them. Cornel's eldest brother, Sandu, grabbed him by the hand and carried him like a small doll. His feet were more in the air than they were on the ground. They ran and ran until finally they were out of the woods and in the safety of the fields. Sadly, they lost most of their hard-won mushrooms while running, but early the next morning they decided to go back and see if they could find any of them, and a useful amount were recovered.

By the early 1970s it became clear to Gheorghe and Maria Lemnariu that the world around them was changing. The communist central powers were now beginning to forcibly spread their tyranny into every corner of Romania. President Nicolae Ceauşescu (a former shoemaker) seemed to have a pathological hatred of the peaceful and self-sufficient village life in the rural parts of Romania. Many say this was because he realised that they could live their lives without him. They didn't want him or need him; they simply wanted to be left alone to live as they had always done for many generations. The communists had confiscated all the land that had originally belonged to the people and anyone who tried to resist the communist authorities was severely punished. Cornel's father tried to resist for a while but in the end he had to give in. Many were killed, put in prison or deported. As the Twentieth Century entered its fourth quarter, Gheorghe and Maria realised that to do even reasonably well in the future, their seven children would need a better education than was available in the local school. Cornel was their youngest and he was showing early signs of being very intelligent. This would need cash!

Their limited cash income was not enough; Gheorghe needed a job with a regular salary. He searched for one, but in their rural environment of northern Moldova jobs were not plentiful and the wages were low. Even the land they cultivated no longer belonged to them. He reluctantly came to the conclusion that he and his family would probably have to relocate to a place where he could find a job. Gheorghe's Uncle Grigore lived in Constanta, Romania's main seaport city on the Black Sea coast. Grigore encouraged him to seek employment in Constanta where more jobs were available. Gheorghe moved initially on his own, and began to search for work in an environment that could not be more different than the farming life he had always known in the north of Moldova. In Constanta he found work running the boiler for the heating system in the basement of a large office block in the city. The work was hot, dirty and underground, but Gheorghe was prepared to do it to earn enough to support his family and educate his children.

Although Gheorghe had moved to Constanta to establish himself several months before his family, Cornel's mother, Maria, was understandably reluctant to make the move and would need some persuading to do so. It seemed like a leap into the unknown from the life that she and her parents had always known. There was a rhythm to rural life that was normal for her. Growing crops, raising animals, feeding the chickens, enduring the fierce winters and raising her children were all she had known. She could see the need for her children's education, but what if things didn't work out? What would they do? She agonised and prayed a lot to the God she had known ever since she could remember.

Her parents were members of The Romanian Orthodox Church, but Maria as a teenager began meeting with their local 'Oastea Domnului' (in English 'The Lord's Army') group. This is an evangelical renewal movement within The Romanian Orthodox Church. It was founded in 1923 by the Orthodox priest Iosif Trifa (1888-1938). After his death the leadership was taken up by Ioan Marini and then Traian Dorz (25th December 1914 – 20th June 1989) who became the movement's leader after Marini's death in 1947. Traian Dorz was undoubtedly one of the greatest leaders the church in Europe has ever had, even though he is little known outside of Romania. He suffered terribly at the hands of the communist regime, spending a total of seventeen years in prison in horrific conditions. Yet he was a prolific writer of thousands of poems, psalms and proverbs. He is revered as Romania's greatest poet.

Over the many years since The Lord's Army began, millions of Romanians have been part of the movement, and Maria Lemnariu was one of them. Her personal commitment to following Christ was foundational to her life. Gheorghe went along to the meetings, but his commitment was more to the Orthodox Church. Most of the Orthodox hierarchy and priests were opposed to The Lord's Army because it challenged their authority. Obedience to Christ's teaching in the Gospels and the New Testament letters were paramount and they refused the authority of the priests whenever the two conflicted. They strongly held to the doctrines of salvation by grace through faith, repentance and the priesthood of all believers. They maintained the basics of the Orthodox priesthood only for baptism, marriage and funerals. They held and continue to hold their own local meetings separate to the Orthodox Church, usually in separate locations and, under the Communists, often in secret. The hierarchy of the Orthodox Church wished that The Lord's Army would leave the church, but they stubbornly refused to do so. The

Lord's Army has always been determined to maintain their membership and presence in the mainstream Orthodox Church whatever the cost. It is true to say that The Lord's Army came under double persecution, from both the Communist government and the Orthodox Church.

In Horlăceni The Lord's Army group had taken to meeting in each other's homes, usually in the afternoon, to allow members to attend their traditional Orthodox service in the morning. This pattern was common for The Lord's Army groups throughout Romania. For Maria, the pressure from the local priest became so restrictive and downright unpleasant that she took the decision to switch to the local and unofficial Apostolic Pentecostal Church for her morning church attendance. There was some tension between Maria and Gheorghe over this move because he really liked the local Orthodox church and did not have the same evangelical convictions as Maria. He had a lay position of some significance in their local church with responsibilities that included ringing the church bell. This was important to him.

Two further issues had brought the subject of the children's education into sharper focus. First, Cornel's older brother Mircea had already moved three hundred kilometres south-west to the large city of Cluj Napoca to further his education. The family had no relatives in Cluj Napoca but Mircea was able to live in accommodation on the school's campus. The second issue was Cornel's obvious intelligence, even at this early stage in his education. He spent a year in Kindergarten at the age of five and it became clear to his teachers that he could already read and write fairly well, though not expertly yet. He had achieved this simply by observing his older siblings as they did their homework. As he was about to start grade one, Cornel began to suffer pain and swelling in his right knee, preventing him from starting school. He was hospitalised for two months in Dorohoi Municipal Hospital about ten kilometres away and treated for rheumatism.

Happily, the treatment was successful and Cornel was now ready to begin school. His mother wanted him to delay starting until the beginning of the next year because he was now two months behind his peers. He would then have the full year and not, as she thought, be disadvantaged by missing the first two months, which are so crucial for children of that age. The school's grade one teacher, Mrs Ciobanu, lived in the same street as Cornel's family and she had a very different idea. Knowing something about Cornel's potential from his time in Kindergarten, she visited the family and insisted that Cornel should begin school immediately, regardless of his late start. Maria reluctantly agreed and Mrs Ciobanu was proved correct when at the end of the Grade One year, Cornel came top of his class!

As for the decision to move to Constanta, Maria knew that in spite of all her doubts, the call of her husband and the possibility of improved opportunities for her children were extremely important. The hardest sticking point for her was her church and her faith. She would not move to a place where she could not practise her Christianity in an evangelical/Pentecostal church – and Gheorghe knew this. Gheorghe's uncle Grigore was a Pentecostal himself and Gheorghe had begun to attend the local Pentecostal church with him. To overcome Maria's reluctance, Gheorghe wrote and promised her that if she made the move, she could go to any church she wanted and he would not object. He also promised that he would join the Pentecostal church too. This tipped the balance and Maria finally agreed to the move, putting aside her doubts and fears.

Once the decision had been made, Gheorghe rented a small house with only two rooms, in the village of Cumpăna, which is situated about ten kilometres south-west of the centre of Constanta. Cumpăna at that time was about half the size it is today. It was small, poor, fairly remote and, as far as most of the world was concerned, unheard of! There was no Pentecostal church in Cumpăna at that time, and until there was, Maria travelled into Constanta to the church where Gheorghe's uncle worshipped. Housing in villages in Romania is generally cheaper than in the large towns. Romanians often find it puzzling that in the United Kingdom, houses situated in villages near a large town are usually more expensive. Thus it was that in 1972 Maria and her children took the leap into the unknown and moved the six hundred kilometres to Cumpăna – where both Maria and Gheorghe were destined to live out the rest of their lives.

Cumpăna

In recent years, Cumpăna has become a popular residential area for the people leaving the crowded city of Constanta. This has resulted in expansion and modernisation. The population has risen to about 14,000 and the area of the village to fifty-one square kilometres. Recent developments have included a proper sewage system, natural gas pipeline grid, proximity to new major hypermarkets, small hotels and several new restaurants. In Cumpăna there are two Orthodox churches, one of which was renovated in 2007, and a new Pentecostal church building, opened in 1991. In 2007, Cumpăna was awarded the honorary title 'European Village' by the European Union delegation in Romania.

CHAPTER THREE

A Painful Life

IN 1972, AGED SEVEN, CORNEL MOVED WITH HIS FAMILY from Horlaceni, Botosani County to Cumpăna, Constanta County. He joined the Grade 2 class in the local school and continued to do well in his studies. The pain and swelling of his right knee became a distant memory. He ran and played with his friends and siblings in the normal way for children of their age around the village. In due course he proceeded to the secondary school at the age of ten, in line with the Romanian education system, and continued to do well at his studies. Then in 1978, at the age of thirteen, the pain and swelling in his right knee occurred again. This time Cornel was admitted to the General Hospital in Constanta, where he remained for a month, and for Cornel, this began many years of pain, hospitals and wrong diagnoses. His medical history is a long and tragic story; but for God's amazing intervention, it is hard to imagine what would have become of him.

After a month, the hospital's diagnosis was that Cornel was suffering from tuberculosis and it was affecting him in his right knee. Tuberculosis is most commonly known as a disease which affects the lungs, but it can occur in other parts of the body. However, it must be stressed that to affect just one knee is very rare. This diagnosis was wrong. Having decided that the problem was tuberculosis, they moved him to a different hospital in Constanta which normally dealt with this condition. When Cornel's condition didn't respond to the treatment, it was decided to move him to the Tuberculosis (Tuberculoza) Hospital for Children, usually abbreviated to TBC and is located in the town of Mangalia, which is Romania's other Black Sea port, situated forty-two kilometres south of Constanta.

This large hospital was staffed with the normal medical teams of surgeons and nurses, but in addition it had a teaching staff to enable the children to continue their education while in hospital. Children from as young as three and up to the age of eighteen could be accommodated long-term there. The hospital had five floors, with the lower four floors each accommodating a different aged group. The youngest were on the ground floor, slightly older children above, and so on up to the fourth floor with the oldest children. The fifth floor was for the medical work and had the operating theatres. In Cornel's ward there were sixteen beds and he was able to study his seventh grade of the Romanian educational system. It helped a lot that he was clever and coped easily with the studies.

The doctors still didn't really know what Cornel's medical condition was and were still regarding it as tuberculosis in his knee. Their solution was to put his right leg in a plaster cast from hip to toes and to keep him in hospital for some thirteen months. While he was in the cast, there was little or no pain, and his main problem was that he was just very bored and uncomfortable. Because his knee was immobilised, preventing it from bending or weight-bearing, the real problem was masked. When eventually they decided to remove the cast and send him home, his problems really began. His knee joint had become very stiff. He was unable to bend it properly and trying to do so caused severe pain. His walking became slow and very painful.

Now aged fourteen, Cornel was old enough to attend high school. The nearest one was the Liceul CRF (Romanian Railways High School) in Constanta where his older brother Jicu was already a student, studying to be a mechanic. Cornel began to study electronics. Getting to the school was an enormous challenge for him. The journey required taking two buses. To reach the first bus he had to walk for half a kilometre and to reach the second bus to the school there was a further walk of two hundred and fifty metres. Fully fit teenagers would take this journey – quite literally – in their stride; but for Cornel it was a nightmare. His walking was very slow and he was in constant pain, especially for the first half hour of walking while his joints loosened a little. His journey to school required him to start out in the early morning, long before his brother Jicu. The summer was very hot and was followed by a particularly severe winter. The bitter cold, and sometimes snow, added to the difficulty of walking. During the worst snow, the buses through Cumpăna stopped running and he had to stay home. His brother was one of those hardy Romanians who walked the ten kilometres through the snow into Constanta to attend his classes. At this point, Cornel was still hoping his condition would improve. The reality was that the year in hospital had done serious long-term damage to his condition – which still had not been correctly diagnosed.

At this stage Cornel was still managing to function, even with the pain. He completed a year plus one term at the high school. During that time, his leg gradually became worse, rather than better as he had hoped. He was still able to help his parents in their field, harvesting the tomatoes and vegetables that most village-dwelling Romanian families usually cultivated. He could even ride his bike, partly because he could push perfectly well with his left leg and a little with his right, and riding a bike meant that the bike took most of his weight. One day in 1980, after completing the first term of his second year at the high school, Cornel was riding his bike round a slippery corner and fell off, landing heavily on his right hip. He was told that he had broken it. Cornel didn't believe this because he was still able to ride his bike home after this minor accident and continued to walk in the same limited way as before.

It was at this point, aged fifteen, that Cornel's life took a dramatic turn for the worse. On the insistence that he had a broken hip, he was admitted again in December 1980 to the TBC children's hospital in Mangalia. This time his plaster cast was extreme. His cast stretched from his chest to his toes on his right side and to just above his knee on the left. He still had some movement in his left knee and this helped a little. There was a section cut out at the rear of the cast to allow him to use a bed pan, but he ate and drank as little as he could to minimise its use which was of course very difficult. He was immobilised and bedridden, and remained in this miserable, uncomfortable and humiliating condition for six boring months. The only compensation was that he was mostly pain-free. The lack of pain probably convinced the doctors that they were doing the right thing and that once he was out of the cast he would probably be all right and his supposed broken hip would have healed. Nothing could have been further from the truth!

After the cast was removed, Cornel's joints were in a much worse condition than before. His movements were further restricted and much more painful. He took the courageous decision to return to the high school to complete his tenth grade in an attempt to continue his education. Now the journey was more difficult and his walking even slower. He needed to begin his painful walk to catch the bus ninety minutes earlier than it would normally take. Virtually any movement now caused pain in all his main joints. This was clearly nothing to do with either tuberculosis or a broken hip, but no one understood his condition. By July 1981 things became so bad that Cornel was bedridden and in constant pain. He feared anyone coming near him. This was the time when the canal linking the River Danube to the Black Sea was under construction. The location of Cumpăna meant that the giant earth-moving trucks 'as big as a house' constantly roared past the village. This caused vibration that seemed like mini earthquakes. The vibration caused extra pain for Cornel every time one of these monster vehicles roared past. The vibration also caused damage to many of the houses in Cumpăna. In the older houses with poor foundations, serious cracks and subsidence appeared. Cornel just lay on his bed, all day and all night, suffering pain and depression, unable to do anything and wondering what the future held for him.

Cornel and his parents were willing to clutch at any straw that they thought might help. The medical path which he had been following seemed to have run its course with no improvement – just an increasing deterioration. Cornel could only hope to find a different hospital and perhaps they would have a solution. In Romania there was a strict demarcation between children and adults when being admitted to hospital. The patient must be eighteen or over to be admitted to any adult hospital, but he was only seventeen at this time. Cornel's father knew one of the doctors at the Port Hospital in Constanta and he asked this doctor to help. The doctor agreed and explained that he would allow Cornel to be admitted to the hospital and then, after a short period, he would refer him to the Eforie Sud hospital in Constanta where they would then have to accept him. This turned out to be true. Cornel was admitted to the Port Hospital, where he stayed for two weeks before being transferred to the Eforie Sud hospital in Constanta. There he was placed under the care of one of the surgeons for treatment. At this stage, despite being in such pain, Cornel felt a guarded optimism that something could be done to help him.

Cornel was a patient in this hospital for the next thirteen months. He was not put in any plaster cast this time and the only treatment was injections of the expensive corticosteroid medicine Diprophos (betamethasone sodium phosphate), which his family was required to pay for. These injections always took the pain away for a while. Throughout his time under this surgeon, Cornel never once had a proper conversation or consultation with him. Yet the surgeon always insisted that he knew what he was doing and Cornel would recover under his treatment. It is a characteristic of the Romanian people – often noticed by visitors – that they have a 'can-do' attitude to any task before them. We could say that they consider that even the problems are 'no problem'. If there is such a thing as a national motto, this would be it for Romania. They are the DIY champions of the world. If they need a church, or a house, or a major vehicle repair, there is always someone that will insist that it is *"No problem!"* This surgeon was a prime example of this attitude. However, as the months went by, Cornel realised that the surgeon was lying to him. The sad reality was that he did not know what Cornel's problem was or how to treat it.

There was a time when the surgeon decided to perform surgery on Cornel's right knee, insisting that he would improve the knee's function. He did this with a local anaesthetic which simply did not work. This one-hour operation was the most painful experience of Cornel's painful life. His cries of pain could be heard for some distance around, even penetrating to another operating theatre some distance away. To add to his frustration, there was no improvement in the knee's condition. To this day he has no idea what the surgeon was attempting to do; nothing was ever explained to him.

Cornel realised that he was in the wrong hospital and that the surgeon overseeing his case simply didn't know what he was doing. He began asking, then insisting, that he be transferred to the CMR (Centru Metodologic de Reumatologie) hospital in Bucharest. He had heard from one of the medical staff that this hospital was much better. As its name implies, it specialised in the area of medicine that Cornel needed – rheumatology. His surgeon was very reluctant to agree to this move. Perhaps it was a matter of pride or even that the hospital and this doctor were more interested in making money from their patients. Cornel's insistence finally overcame the surgeon's reluctance to admit that he couldn't help him and he wanted to discharge him. Cornel protested vehemently that he didn't want to just to go home; he wanted a transfer to the other hospital. The reason for this was that it could take many months of waiting for a new referral. His insistence paid off. He received the referral he needed for transfer and after a short visit home he was transferred.

The CMR hospital in Bucharest was very different. The doctors were friendly, competent and communicated well with Cornel. Finally, in

1983, at the age of eighteen and after years of pain, hospitals and erroneous treatment, Cornel was at last given the correct diagnosis of his condition. It took the doctors at this hospital only a few days to recognise the degenerative disease ankylosing spondylitis – for which there is no medical cure.

What is ankylosing spondylitis (AS)?

AS is a long-term (chronic) condition in which the spine and other areas of the body become inflamed. AS tends to first develop in teenagers and young adults and is more common in men.

The symptoms of AS can vary, but usually involve back pain, increasing stiffness and deteriorating mobility of the joints. It can cause overgrowth of the bones, which may lead to abnormal joining of bones, called 'bony fusion'. Fusion affects bones of the neck, back, knees or hips, and may impair a person's ability to perform routine activities. Fusion of the ribs to the spine or breastbone may limit a person's ability to expand his or her chest when taking a deep breath. Pain and swelling may occur in other parts of the body – caused by inflammation of the joints.

These symptoms tend to develop gradually, usually over several months or years. In some people the condition gets better with time, but for others it usually gets slowly worse.

It's not known what causes the condition, but it's thought to be genetic. There is no cure for AS and it's not possible to reverse the damage caused by the condition. However, treatment is available to relieve the symptoms and help prevent or delay its progression.

In most cases treatment involves a combination of physiotherapy to reduce stiffness and medication to help relieve pain and reduce inflammation. Corticosteroids have a powerful anti-inflammatory effect and can be taken as tablets or injections. Surgery is sometimes needed to repair significantly damaged joints or correct severe bends in the spine.

If a particular joint is inflamed, corticosteroids can be injected directly into the joint. It's usually considered wise to have an injection up to three times in one year, with at least three months between injections in the same joint.

The doctors at Foisor Orthopaedic Hospital did their best for Cornel, but they didn't have today's modern equipment, medication or training, and the correct diagnosis had come very late in the deterioration of his condition. The various treatments that he had previously been given had mostly made things worse. It was believed that life expectancy for anyone with this condition was no more than thirty years. It was not the custom at that time in Romania to break such bad news directly to patients. One of the doctors told one of Cornel's brothers (Cornel was now aged eighteen) the news that Cornel was not expected to live beyond thirty. Eventually, this devastating news was passed on to Cornel. Modern research has concluded that there are many factors and treatments that govern the life expectancy of AS patients. None of this research was available to Cornel or his doctors at that time. They began treating him with steroids and anti-inflammatory medication. He felt much better with this treatment and left this hospital after one month.

Because ankylosing spondylitis is a degenerative disease, as the following years passed by, and in spite of the medication, Cornel's condition gradually deteriorated and his hip and knee joints became less mobile. By now he could only move around with the aid of crutches. The most difficult condition was his hips. Being unable to bend at the hips meant that he couldn't sit at a table or in a car. He spent his days and nights lying on his bed. Between 1983 and 1989 Cornel attended the CMR hospital in Bucharest every year for about one month each time for the doctors to examine him and observe the extent of his deteriorating condition. To slow down the deterioration, they referred him a number of times to the Foisor Orthopaedic Hospital, also in Bucharest, for surgery. This was the top orthopaedic hospital in Romania. In 1987 he had a right hip replacement which gave him some limited mobility in that joint. In 1988 he had a right knee replacement which at first helped and he could move it about forty-five degrees, though it was very painful to do so. In 1989 Cornel had two operations on his right knee to straighten and align it. Later in 1989 he had a third operation on the right knee which didn't improve its condition.

As 1989 was drawing towards the Christmas celebrations, Cornel was where he seemed to spend so much of his life: in Foisor Orthopaedic Hospital. In late December 1989 he was not getting much attention from the medical staff. Romania's revolution had begun! Immediately before and after the revolution the doctors in this hospital and the other hospitals in Bucharest were overwhelmed with the task of treating the many protestors who were admitted with injuries and gunshot wounds. As a consequence of the situation, Cornel was sent home about a month after the revolution and told to return later. He was again admitted in

May 1990, stayed another six months without any further treatment and was eventually sent home.

It was a frustrating time for Cornel. The hospital kept promising further surgery and even setting a date for it, then cancelling it time after time. There would always be some excuse for the cancellation and the excuses began to sound less and less plausible. It seemed to Cornel like the end of the road. The best doctors that Romania had to offer had given up on him. His future looked bleak and very depressing.

Chapter Four

Known to God

ONE OF THE CHARACTERISTICS OF THE CHURCHES IN Romania, that is often noticed by Christians from the West when they travel there, is that it is usual for several generations of the same family – sometimes large families – to be members of the same church. This is normal, expected and traditional in Romanian culture.

In recent years, of course, many young Romanians have travelled far and wide in search of work. The undeniable fact is that the Romanians who have the energy and initiative to make such a move are usually young, ambitious, intelligent and hard-working. This makes then an attractive proposition for potential employers. But even if the younger generations have moved away from home or even to another country to find jobs, their faith tends to remain intact. Hence there are numerous Romanian-speaking churches in Western countries, catering for the many Romanians who have migrated seeking a better life and employment prospects. In contrast to this, it is too often the case in the West that in spite of the prayers of their parents, too many children brought up in Christian churchgoing families drift away from their parents' faith and fail to find their own personal relationship with God. Of course, this is not true of all, but the contrast between the two cultures in this aspect is stark. The reasons for this are a mystery to most parents and have spawned many books, conferences and seminars on the problems facing teenagers and students choosing to leave the Christian life behind. What cannot be denied is that God has no grandchildren, only children!

Cornel Lemnariu could certainly be regarded as someone who had plenty of reasons to be angry with God! If his ankylosing spondylitis had been diagnosed much earlier – as it should have been – his life would have been very different. If the various 'treatments', the endless months in hospital and the incredible lengths of time in plaster casts, had been the correct procedures, he might have been spared much of the pain and disability that has sadly been his lot and blighted his young life. Sometimes he cried out to God with tears, but through it all, he never blamed God. Did God have a plan for his life? If so, was this the plan? If only Almighty God, the great physician, had heard and answered his prayers…

His mother had always remained close to him. She nursed him and helped him in every way she could and faithfully prayed for him. In his darkest days of pain and wondering if life would ever be better, surely anyone would have understood if he had blamed God and lost his faith. But the fact is that he didn't. His faith in God remained strong even though it was sorely tested all through the confusion and mistreatment at the hands of doctors who simply did not have the training and knowledge that was required. His mother Maria was an excellent role model. She continually demonstrated her faith to her children, daily praying with them and for them, teaching them the Bible. Cornel understood that the overall context of his life was that Christians at that time in Romania were under general persecution and discrimination. They did their best to live in peace as long as they could do so without compromising their faith in Christ. If their life was difficult then so be it. Jesus himself predicted that following Him would carry a cost.

Cornel was not happy at school, where he and his brothers were bullied by other children and treated badly by some of the teachers. They had to endure this because they couldn't do much to defend themselves at that time. But eventually there were three of them together, and then his brother Viorel would begin to fight back at the bullies and even overcome them. He looked after Cornel and protected him during their time in primary school. When they went to secondary school, one of the teachers began to punish them because of their faith. There was no other apparent reason for it. They would sometimes be beaten or made to stand for hours in the classroom in front of all the other pupils – and this was just because they were Christians. This was part of the communist culture of discouraging children from following any religious faith.

Cornel did have one teacher that he liked though; he was Mr Pacala who taught French. Cornel was the best at French in the class and Mr Pacala would only ask him to answer a question if no one else knew the answer. Cornel did have a bit of an advantage because his older brothers and sisters had all been learning French at school and would often converse in French at home, so he picked it up from them. It was very useful for them to be able to speak in French every time they wanted to talk about something that they didn't want their parents to know about. The fact is that Christians expected to face persecution and were prepared to pay the cost. This strengthened their faith as only persecution can. When Cornel became confined for most of the time to his bed, he had the opportunity to read a lot. One of the things he did was to read the whole Bible more than twice. In it he was impressed by the story of Job and his suffering. For Cornel suffering was an accepted part of the Christian life and although he could become angry with doctors, hospitals, the poor health service and the frustration of not being able to move around easily, he never blamed God.

In 1972, when Cornel, at the age of seven, moved with his family from Botosani County to Cumpăna, there was no Pentecostal church in the village. But Cornel's father, Gheorghe, kept his promise to Maria and allowed her to attend the one in Constanta. Most of the time, Maria took only the older children with her to church because the bus fares for the whole family were just too expensive for them. Gheoghe's faith was not very strong, but he occasionally accompanied them.

Their first home in Cumpăna was a rented house with just two rooms for a family of nine. Even in a culture that was accustomed to multiple occupants sharing a bedroom and one room having to serve several purposes, this was very crowded. However, it was all they could afford and it had to do for a while. In true Romanian style, Gheorghe and Maria purchased a plot of land (about four hundred square metres) on the edge of the village and began building their own house. They engaged an architect to draw up plans according to their own specifications. Once they had gained planning permission, they began work. After four months they moved again and rented another slightly larger house which was conveniently near their own plot of land. They lived for a further four months at this second house. During those months, the whole family worked hard building their own house. Even Cornel, who was the youngest, worked alongside the rest of his family. They even made their own blocks out of yellow mud and straw (about 40 cm long, 22 cm wide and 13 cm in height). Wooden moulds were used to form the blocks, which were then left to dry in the hot summer sun. The same mud was used to plaster the walls. They dug foundations and built the walls up to roof level, and then they needed the services of a professional carpenter to add the roof beams and the roofing. When the roof was only partially in place, they began to move in. It was the summer of 1973 and if part of the roof was still not in place, it didn't matter much. Occasionally it rained and some things got wet, but they didn't care; they were moving in! They had a well in the garden for their water supply and a few months later the electricity was installed.

Maria wanted a house that would be suitable for meetings and this was the driving force behind the design of this single-storey home. Gheorghe's uncle Grigore in Constanta was good at building and he advised them. Christians in the village were already meeting discretely in each other's homes in small groups of fifteen to twenty. Maria wanted a house that could accommodate larger groups, and secrecy from the authorities and the Securitate (secret police) was an important factor. The design had security built into it. There were three bedrooms, a small kitchen and a large lounge for meetings. The toilet was outside in the garden, which was normal for rural villages. Maria grew some vegetables and they owned a few animals which they had brought with them from Horlaceni. The bedrooms screened the larger room from outside view. There was only one small window in the lounge and that faced outward away from the village.

Over the next few years the size of the meetings grew and they were not held in the same place every week. They moved the meetings from one house to another. The location of the next meeting was never openly announced but was communicated during the week by word of mouth for security reasons. Religious meetings in homes were not allowed and Christians who insisted on doing this ran the constant risk of incurring persecution and penalties from the Securitate. Cornel was often one of the messengers sent to help spread the information. Most of the congregation lived in Cumpăna, but others travelled in from outlying communities by bus or bicycle to attend the meetings. An evening meeting that began at eight o'clock usually lasted until eleven or twelve o'clock and this was usually after a hard day's work. Even with the larger lounge, it was not enough for the growing needs of the group. When the lounge filled up, the bedrooms were there to act as overflow rooms and the meeting continued with all the bedroom doors open so everyone could hear or be heard.

Eventually the much larger 'mother' Pentecostal church in Constanta, under the leadership of Pastor Nicu Topciu, decided that the Cumpăna group needed their own pastor. They chose a very good and well-respected member of the group, Vasile Ungureanu. He was particularly helpful to Cornel, who had to travel so often for hospital appointments in Bucharest. Public transport was available but it was difficult, slow and expensive. Cornel had to walk to the bus stop and at the Bucharest end get to the hospital. Vasile had a Dacia 1300 car and often offered to drive him to Bucharest for his appointment. Bucharest was about two hundred and fifty kilometres from Cumpăna, making it a slow five-hundred-kilometre round trip[1] on a winding road through numerous villages. At that time there was no autostrada (motorway, autobahn) as there is today.

As part of the severe austerity measures that Ceauşescu imposed from 1985, petrol was rationed to a miserly seventeen litres per month! (In Bucharest the monthly petrol allowance was forty litres per month.) Also, on Sundays driving was restricted to odd registration number plates one week and even numbers the following Sunday. To help Cornel, Vasile and Cornel's brother Viorel pooled their petrol resources by saving up petrol coupons to make possible the journey to Bucharest, which required forty litres. Even if Romanians had petrol coupons, petrol was scarce. The motorists queued up for hours, sometimes days, before their local 'Peco' station had a delivery of petrol to sell, even though Romania had its own petroleum industry. This was evidenced by the many oil wells with their 'nodding donkeys' dotted over the landscape in many parts of Romania for all to see.

In 1978 the Christians of Cumpăna took a courageous step and established their first permanent church building. One of the families removed an internal wall between two rooms in their house and created a room that was about eight metres long by four metres wide. The house was only five years old and was therefore in good condition. The local Securitate kept threatening them about this, but Pastor Vasile researched the Romanian laws and constitution on this subject and discovered that officially there was supposed to be freedom of religion. He printed the quotation out and posted it on the wall of the building. This inhibited the authorities from overtly opposing the church, and perhaps gave them an excuse to do nothing. After all, the Christians were generally keeping a

---

[1] three hundred and ten miles

low profile and not causing any trouble. The one person that really opposed the church was the local Orthodox priest, who saw it as competition to his own church.

The new space could accommodate about sixty adults and their children for services. Only some of the members had Bibles. Cornel was thirteen when the church opened, but it was not until 1981, when he was sixteen, that he received his first Bible. In the West, church services are comparatively short and people tend to get irritated if the meeting goes beyond the expected time. In Cumpăna the Sunday morning service was three hours long and the Sunday evening service lasted two hours. This was quite normal for non-Orthodox churches throughout Romania. On Wednesday evenings they had a two-hour service and on Friday evening a one-hour prayer meeting. After the revolution, in common with many churches in Romania, the Christians in Cumpăna began construction of a larger building at a pace the church could financially afford. This building is more recognisable as a church building and is about twenty metres by eight metres. It was completed in 1995 and later they added a balcony. This new church can easily accommodate a hundred adults and lots of children.

In 1984, and after being finally diagnosed correctly with ankylosing spondylitis, Cornel was given medication (which he had to purchase) that eased enough of the pain to allow him to move around a little better on his crutches. He began to think what he might do to bring some income in for the family and help with the cost of his medication. He decided to try photography, so he purchased a low-cost camera and the equipment for developing black-and-white photos in an improvised dark room that he set up in his house. At that time in rural Romania, hardly anyone owned their own cameras. He was soon in demand to take photographs of families, weddings and especially the identity (ID) cards required by the government for all citizens. He developed them himself and charged much less than the other two photographers in Cumpăna. Customers liked that they could just turn up at Cornel's door, have their photograph taken and developed, all done in an hour, at half the usual cost.

In December 1984 their pastor Vasile went to the United States on a visitor's visa, sponsored by his relatives who already lived there. After being there for about a year, he had permission to stay permanently. He was then eventually able to arrange for his wife and ten children to join him. This was unusual at the time, but sponsorship in dollars and the fact that he had to leave behind their house, probably helped. It may also be that the communist authorities didn't mind getting rid of Christian ministers and pastors! Vasile was an engineer by profession but he was also a keen amateur photographer and had all the equipment for developing colour photographs plus a good camera. Once he realised that he was going to stay in the United States, he told his wife to give all his equipment and the camera to Cornel. This really boosted Cornel's photography business and enabled him to earn a modest but vital income. It wasn't always easy to get the supplies for developing the colour photographs, but with the help of his brothers driving him around to other places such as Constanta, he always managed to continue the work and became the most popular photographer in Cumpăna. He knew the local police chief well, who always sent customers to him for the ID photographs. In one year alone, he produced about five hundred ID prints. The business only trailed off after the revolution, when Western goods became available and people started to buy their own digital cameras.

The small village of Cumpăna was virtually unknown to the outside world. Most of Romania would never have heard of this place. It was just a dot on the map and one of the many small rural villages in Romania. But God has a plan for the lives of all His children, even if they don't understand it. Cornel certainly couldn't understand at that time how his life would unfold or how the grace of God would intervene in his difficult situation. But God was about to prove that 'the God who counts the number of the stars and calls them all by name' knew everything about Cornel, his family, his church and indeed the whole of Romania; and in His great love He cared about them all, whatever their situation.

1989: The Year the World Changed

Mikhail Gorbachev, General Secretary of the Communist Party of the Soviet Union, began a process which led to the dissolution of the Soviet Union in December 1991, resulting in ten new countries (Armenia, Azerbaijan, Belarus, Georgia, Kazakhstan, Moldova, Tajikistan, Turkmenistan, Ukraine and Uzbekistan). They declared their independence from the Soviet Union. The Baltic States (Estonia, Latvia, and Lithuania) regained their independence.

The rest of the Soviet Union became the Russian Federation in December 1991.

5th February: Sky Television was launched

24th March: The worst oil spill in US history occurred, when the super-tanker Exxon Valdez ran aground in Alaska, spilling an incredible 35,000 metric tons of crude oil.

2nd May: Hungary removed its border fence.

3rd June: Ayatollah Khomeini, the supreme leader of the Islamic Republic of Iran, died aged eighty-six.

5th June: In Poland the Solidarity movement won the first free election, by an overwhelming majority.

5th June: In China pro-democracy rallies in Tiananmen Square ended when soldiers opened fire on demonstrators, killing many.

10th September: Hungary opened its borders allowing thousands of East Germans to leave for the West.

17th October: An earthquake hit San Francisco measuring 6.9 on the Richter scale; fifty-seven died.

9th November: The Berlin Wall came down.

17th November: 'The Velvet Revolution' in Czechoslovakia, led by Vaclav Havel, commenced.

20th December: US troops invaded Panama. The President, General Manuel Noriega, was arrested and imprisoned.

21st December: The Lancaster House Agreement recognised the Republic of Zimbabwe.

22nd December: Revolution in Romania deposed Nicolae and Elana Ceauşescu. They were executed on 25th.

CHAPTER FIVE

The Devil's Left Hand

IN THE HISTORY OF THE HUMAN RACE, THERE IS A LONG LIST of evil tyrants who gain power by fair means or foul and then use that power to oppress, corrupt and commit unspeakable crimes of cruelty, often on a massive scale. Some Bible commentators say that the first of these was probably Nimrod, who built the city of Babylon, the tower of Babel and the city of Nineveh.[2] In 1887 Lord Acton famously wrote, "Power tends to corrupt and absolute power corrupts absolutely." The stock-in-trade of tyrants is violence, torture, genocide, corruption and megalomania. This is inevitably manifested in a ruthless personality cult that allows no criticism and insists on a manifested sycophantic adulation from everyone under their control. They seek to assume a god-like status and usually ensure that their photographs are displayed everywhere. Their latest so-called achievements dominate the media which they control. From the time of Julius Caesar, the emperors of the Roman Empire required the whole of the population to worship them as gods, after or even before they died. It was the Emperor Domitian (who reigned AD 81-96) who tortured Christians and then executed them for refusing to burn incense to him as an annual act of worship. In the centuries that followed, the records – limited as they are – of tyrants such as Attila the Hun (AD 406-453) and Genghis Khan (1162-1227) show that they attempted to conquer the then-known world and slaughtered many thousands of people indiscriminately in pursuing their ungodly aims.

In the Twentieth Century, even allowing for the fact that we had more extensive records and saturating media coverage to expose everything, we could perhaps call this period 'the century of the tyrants'. In addition

---

[2] See Genesis 10:8-12

to the tyrants' regimes, we also had tyrannical movements which were religion-based. Examples of these are Muslim and Hindu extremist groups that have killed and injured many thousands. But religious extremism is nothing new. The Crusades (1095-1291) and the Spanish Inquisition (1478-1834) are examples of religiously inspired evil. In the Twentieth Century we also have seen the rise of politically motivated tyrants. Although their motivation may have been purely political at the outset of their careers, once in power they developed into individual despots. The notable characteristics or the generalisation of their power structure usually fell into one of two types, usually categorised as extreme 'right-wing' or extreme 'left-wing'. Although these regimes seemingly occupy opposite ends of the political spectrum, they exhibit remarkably similar characteristics of evil, cruelty, corruption and megalomania. It seems that the Devil has a right hand and a left hand!

The Four Freedoms

On 6th January 1941, United States President Franklin D. Roosevelt, in his annual State of the Union address and while Adolf Hitler's armies were raging across Europe, summarised the philosophy that has underpinned free democratic societies ever since. They have become known simply as the 'Four Freedoms':
1. Freedom of speech.
2. Freedom of worship.
3. Freedom from want.
4. Freedom from fear.

Later, they were incorporated into the preamble to the 'United Nations Universal Declaration of Human Rights'.

Historians have estimated the number of human deaths attributed to individual despots, but their crimes also include many more unnumbered victims of imprisonment, hunger, beatings, torture and families devastated by poverty and the loss of family members. Heading the Devil's right-hand list is Adolf Hitler (1889-1945) with thirty million deaths attributed to him as a result of the Second World War which he initiated, and including the genocide of six million Jews. His secret police were the dreaded Gestapo. Closely allied with him was the Italian fascist dictator Benito Mussolini (1882-1945). Other extreme right-wing dictators with the blood of many on their hands were leaders such as

Spain's fascist dictator Francisco Franco, a Spanish general who ruled over Spain as a military dictator from 1939 until his death in 1975. General Pinochet was a military dictator who came to power in Chile through a *coup d'état* in 1973 and through his notorious 'death squads' murdered, imprisoned and tortured thousands of his political opponents. To this list of right-wing infamy we should add Saddam Hussein of Iraq, Muammar Gaddafi of Libya, Uganda's comical but brutal Idi Amin Dada (1925-2003) who was given sanctuary and a generous pension in Saudi Arabia until his death (he was, after all, a Muslim) and Iran's 'Revolutionary Guard Corp', under the leadership of a succession of Ayatollahs (supreme leaders) whose purpose is supporting the extreme Shiite Islamic regime and enforcing the observance of their strict religious codes.

Top of the all-time list of the Devil's left hand is the greatest mass murderer in history, China's so-called 'Great Helmsman', Mao Zedong. He is estimated to be responsible for the deaths of fifty to seventy million people – mostly his own citizens. In addition to this, his inept mismanagement of the economy and the political upheavals he launched ensured a climate of fear and a life of poverty for hundreds of millions in China. He is followed on the list by Joseph Stalin (1878-1953), founder of the Union of Soviet Socialist Republics (USSR). This consolidated the power of Russia over Eastern and Central Europe after the Second World War. He is estimated to be responsible for the deaths of forty million victims. He used starvation on a vast scale as a political weapon. The Soviet Union used what are now called 'proxy wars' as they attempted to spread communism around the world.

These were aided by other communist states such as Fidel Castro's Cuba, Kim Ilsung's North Korea and the Cambodian genocide which was carried out by the Khmer Rouge regime under the leadership of Pol Pot, killing up to three million Cambodian people from 1975 to 1979. In other countries, puppet Marxist regimes were established in places such as Angola and Mozambique in southern Africa. Here too, millions were either killed, injured or fled their country as refugees. Deaths and injuries continued in these countries long after the civil wars ceased, from countless anti-personnel mines which took years to clear.

A number of European countries were overrun by Russian forces at the end of the Second World War and communist regimes were set up, either by force or the threat of force, to establish 'The Warsaw Pact', a political and military alliance that threatened to take over the rest of

Europe. These countries included Poland, East Germany, Czechoslovakia, Bulgaria, Albania, Hungary and Romania. It was established on 14th May 1955 in the Polish Capital of Warsaw. Each of these countries, as with all totalitarian regimes, built a powerful secret police organisation that suppressed any opposition or criticism of their country's dictatorial regimes or their policies. Their methods of repression included spying on their citizens and employing violence, intimidation, incarceration and murder to enforce the will of the regime and engender fear in the population. Their *modus operandi* employed torture, beatings, economic discrimination, denial of human rights and threats to their victims' family and friends.

Among the most notorious and brutal of these organisations are Adolf Hitler's 'Gestapo', Mao Zedong's 'Hongweibing' (which didn't need to be secret; it was open, brutal and feared), Russia's 'KGB' (Committee for State Security) and its successor the 'FSB' (Federal Security Service). East Germany (German Democratic Republic) had what is regarded as the most effective of these organs of repression, the 'Ministry for State Security' commonly known as the 'Stasi'. Most countries have some sort of secret service and security agencies as part of their national security structure (the United States has seventeen). They are expected to gather information on their enemies, real or potential. Spying is often referred to as 'the second oldest profession'. It is not the existence of such organisations that must be scrutinised or held to account, but it is the nature of the regimes, the level of freedom they deny their people and the despotic leaders they support. There is, however, one more in the Devil's left hand we should add to the catalogue of infamy listed above and that is 'Romania's Ministry of State Security' – simply known as the 'Securitate'.

Cornel Lemnaru was born and raised in a country which was dominated by this evil, much-feared organisation, wielded by Nicolae Ceaușescu after he came to power to ruthlessly oppress Romania's people and bolster his inflated ego. The Securitate was founded in August 1948 and dissolved in 1989 after the revolution. Although Romania was part of the Warsaw Pact, Ceaușescu wanted to preserve semi-independence from it. He was aware though that on 31st October 1956, under the new leadership of Nikita Khrushchev, Russian T-54 tanks had rolled into Hungary to ruthlessly put down a popular uprising which demanded independence from Soviet control. More than 2,500 Hungarians were killed and 200,000 fled their country as refugees. Then, in what became known as 'The Prague Spring' (January-August 1968), Czechoslovakia attempted to break free of the Soviet stranglehold and implement popular reforms. The revolt was led by students and intellectuals. Again, the Russians (now led by Leonid Brezhnev) deployed their tanks to crush any thoughts of independence. Thus they underlined again that Soviet rule, and their communist doctrines, only ever maintained their rule by military force. Their power only ever came from the barrel of a gun! The Czech intellectuals were redeployed from their jobs in universities to menial jobs where they had no one to talk to, such as window cleaning and stoking boilers in basements. No wonder they took to renaming their country as 'Absurdistan'.

Therefore, Ceaușescu needed to tread carefully lest he upset the Soviets and the fate of Hungary and Czechoslovakia befell him too. There was, however, an important difference in Romania, and that was the iron stranglehold which the Securitate had on the whole country. He tried, with some success, to face both ways. He could assure his Soviet comrades that no students or intellectuals would ever try to exert political power; they just wouldn't dare. At the same time, he flirted with the Western governments, creating the idea that he was a free spirit and wouldn't necessarily always toe the Soviet line. This led to the bizarre invitation for him to enjoy a state visit to the United Kingdom in June 1978 and even stay in Buckingham Palace. He sat next to the Queen in an open carriage riding down London's Mall, waving to the crowds. Perhaps he thought that the crowds were waving back to him, when actually they were more likely waving to the Queen.

Romania became a prison, incarcerating its population. Special people, such as some of the party hierarchy or international-level athletes, were given permission to travel abroad, but there was always the fear that they might 'defect'. For the ordinary citizens, trying to escape the country was considered so serious a crime that you could be shot by border guards if you were seen trying to leave. The same was true of some other communist countries. An example of this was of course the 'Berlin Wall'. There could hardly be a more damning judgment of any political system by its own citizens than the fact that if they wanted to leave, or even visit other countries, they were not allowed, and severe penalties were imposed on anyone unauthorised who tried to do so. Romania's Securitate could match or exceed most of their fellow secret police organisations for their brutality, intimidation and their ubiquitous penetration of the Romanian population. The Securitate was, in proportion to Romania's population, one of the largest secret police forces in the Eastern bloc. At its height, the Securitate employed some eleven thousand agents and had half a million informers for a country with a population of twenty-two million. Many of the informers were either intimidated or threatened into the role, and some saw it as a way to gain materially to alleviate their poverty and provide a slightly better life for their families.

Under Ceaușescu, the Securitate was one of the most brutal secret police forces in the world, responsible for the arrests, torture and deaths of thousands of people. The first widespread revelations of the Securitate's oppression of Christians, in particular, came when Richard Wurmbrand (1909-2001), who had spent fourteen years in prison, published his book, *Tortured for Christ*, which sold in the millions all over the world. In May 1966, he testified before the U.S. Senate Internal Security Subcommittee, where he stripped to the waist to show eighteen shocking scars from torture wounds covering his torso. His story was carried in newspapers throughout the U.S., Europe and Asia. His writings were translated into sixty languages and he founded his own mission organisation, 'Voice of the Martyrs', which, with other organisations such as 'Open Doors', 'The Slavic Gospel Association' and 'The Romanian Missionary Society', campaigned on behalf of Christians oppressed in communist countries around the world. This led to concerted campaigns to support Romanian Christians imprisoned and ill-treated for their Christian faith, and to numerous successful operations to covertly import Bibles and other Christian books into the country by Western couriers.

There are many stories of courageous Romanian Christians who suffered for their faith at the hands of Ceaușescu's Securitate and never gave up. Some died, some were scarred for life, and countless others coped by living their lives as quietly as they could under daily oppression. Just one example will have to briefly represent them all by way of illustration. Alex (not his real name) was a brave covert distributer of many Bibles in his homeland of Romania. Eventually he was caught and brutally interrogated by the Securitate. They wanted to know where the Bibles came from, but he refused to tell them. In one of the many and more bizarre types of interrogation that he endured, he was locked in a small room with a large ferocious dog. He was told that if he stood on one leg the dog would not attack him. If he put his other foot down the dog was trained to attack him. He could escape this treatment if he gave up the information that the Securitate wanted. His interrogators didn't return to the room for three hours! We might well ask what kind of sick mind thinks up such a method and trains a dog to do this.

Eventually Alex was sentenced to ten years in prison. A Western mission organised a mass letter-writing campaign which resulted in over ten thousand letters being written to him, assuring him of their prayers and support. The Romanian authorities were embarrassed and fearful of the adverse publicity this was generating. Their solution was to strip Alex, his wife and their four children of their Romanian citizenship and expel them from the country, after he had served less than a year in jail. As the prison released him, Alex was asked if he would like to take his mail with him. He said he would, until he saw a small storeroom piled high with his thousands of letters from the West. He had no idea that any of these had been sent. He just told them that they could keep them.

Alex and his family travelled by train and eventually arrived at a refugee camp in West Germany late at night. They were given a small apartment and thirty Deutschmarks per person, including their four children. One hundred and fifty Deutschmarks represented a small fortune to them. They were told that the next morning they could go to the local supermarket and buy food for the family. Alex and his wife went the next morning to buy some breakfast of bread and cheese. This was the first time they had been out of Romania and so they had never seen a Western supermarket. In Romania there was little or nothing in the shops and people queued for bread. Their first surprise was the supermarket doors opening automatically as they approached. Once inside they were shocked to see about twenty types of bread and many types of cheese to choose from. After gazing round for a few minutes, Alex's wife burst into tears and ran out of the supermarket. It was two weeks before she could be persuaded to return. She said something that serves to illustrate her confused emotions: "Are they so good that they have so much; and are we so bad that we have so little?"

A Palace Fit for a Tyrant

It was meant to be Ceaușescu's greatest achievement and embellish his megalomaniacal ego. Initially, it was named 'House of the Republic', but its name was changed after the revolution into 'People's House'. When it became the headquarters of the Senate and Chamber of Deputies, it was again renamed as the 'Palace of the Parliament'. The construction process involved four hundred architects and they were coordinated by a young woman aged twenty-eight named Anca Petrescu.

The Palace is the second-largest administrative building in the world after the Pentagon, with a height of eighty-four metres, an area of 365,000 square metres and a volume of 2,550,000 cubic metres. In terms of weight, the Palace of the Parliament is the heaviest building in the world, weighing in at around 4,098,500,000 kilograms. Construction of the Palace began on June 25th, 1984, but Ceaușescu was executed when it was only two thirds complete. The Palace sinks by 6 mm each year due to its massive weight and is large enough to be visible from the moon.

This colossal building, known for its ornate interior, houses the Senate and the Chamber of Deputies, three museums and an international conference centre, but even so, about 70% of the building remains empty. Only four hundred out of 1,100 rooms are used. About a third of the old city centre was ruthlessly demolished to make way for it. Many historic buildings were lost. Forty thousand people were forcibly displaced. The Brancovenesc Hospital, which was one of Romania's best, was also demolished. Some of the doctors moved to the Foisor Hospital.

The works were carried out with forced labour of soldiers and so-called 'volunteers'. Between 20,000 and 100,000 people worked on the site at various stages, sometimes operating in three shifts each day. An estimated 3,000 construction workers died and many more were injured due to appalling safety standards. In 2006 the building costs were estimated at three billion euros. The building has eight underground levels, the last one being a nuclear bunker, linked to the main state institutions by twenty kilometres of catacombs and tunnels. These were designed by Ceaușescu to get from the building to the airport below ground in case of a revolution. As events proved, the tunnels didn't do him any good.

Chapter Six

Local Heroes

THE TITLE OF THIS CHAPTER IS TAKEN FROM THE FILM OF the same name. The message of the film is that big things can be achieved by little or unimportant people. This is best explained by 1 Corinthians 1:27-29.[3] God can use seemingly unimportant people to do important things in His kingdom if He so chooses – and He often does!

In September of the momentous year of 1989, the Open Doors mission to the persecuted church around the world began a programme of offering 'motivational trips', also known as 'Friendship Tours', for prayer partners and supporters, to some of the countries into which they ministered. The first of these was in September of that year. It was a bus tour to Czechoslovakia, just one week before their Velvet Revolution led by playwright Václav Havel, who then became President. This trip was organised and led by John and Grace Miles, when John was working for Open Doors.

Such trips to Romania were not possible until after their revolution of 22nd December. It was the year when everything began to change. Initially, the most significant change was that the once closed and restrictive borders were now open and visitors from the West were now welcome. Importantly, the Bible was no longer a banned book and could be taken openly across the border. Open Doors were quick off the mark, and in May 1990 a consignment of 100,000 Romanian-language Bibles

---

[3] 1 Corinthians 1:27-29: 'But God has chosen the foolish things of the world to put to shame the wise, and God has chosen the weak things of the world to put to shame the things which are mighty; and the base things of the world and the things which are despised God has chosen, and the things which are not, to bring to nothing the things that are, that no flesh should glory in His presence.'

had been printed and delivered by truck to the central town of Mediaş. From there, over the next two weeks, they were delivered by four Volkswagen vans in smaller quantities (usually three to four hundred) to churches and contacts all over Romania. One of the more distant destinations was to Pastor Nicu, leader of the Pentecostal church in Constanta, on the Black Sea coast. This van was driven by two Open Doors British staff, John Miles and Revd Don Boyes.

In the summer of 1989 Cornel decided that he wanted to learn English. It was six months before the revolution and Cornel had no obvious reason to do this. Travel was still forbidden, he was severely handicapped, and he lived in a small, remote rural village ten kilometres from the nearest town of Constanta. Cornel had a friend who had a 'Teach Yourself English' book, so he asked if he could borrow it for two weeks and his friend agreed. Cornel obviously knew that he couldn't learn English in two weeks, so he began to copy the book, which had about four hundred pages, by hand, into exercise books. After many hours of copying every day, by the end of the two weeks he had his own copy of the book. He was ridiculed by others for learning English because no one could see any purpose for it. Some said he was mad. Nevertheless, he was determined, and given time, persistence and his innate intelligence, he made remarkable progress. He didn't realise it at the time, but this was to prove very important for his future. It would be a vital stepping-stone into a whole new world.

Now that the Romanian borders were open, the way was clear for Open Doors to organise a Friendship Tour there for prayer partners. This happened in September 1990, only eight months after the revolution. The group of about thirty-five flew to Constanta (from Manchester on a charter flight), where a tour bus met them at the airport. They stayed a few days in the beach-front Savoy Hotel in the Mamaia area of Constanta, about eight kilometres north of the city centre, before the bus took them on to the Lebădă (Swan) Hotel in Bucharest. Unfortunately, as with so much in Romania under Ceauşescu's corrupt and incompetent regime, most of the hotels and other facilities for tourists were neglected, run down and below the most basic standard needed for international tourists. This was most evident in Constanta, which was traditionally a popular holiday destination on the Black Sea coast, as well as Romania's main seaport.

This group of visitors were prepared to put up with this because they were not there for a luxury holiday; they had their own motives for signing up for what turned out to be a difficult tour. For about two years following the revolution, Romania offered package holidays which appeared in some of the holiday brochures in Western Europe. The holiday companies in the United Kingdom soon dropped Romania from their brochures because of the deluge of complaints from customers, mainly about the poor food that they were served. Things are very different now; Romania is an excellent place for holidays and has a lot to offer for skiing in the winter, beaches in the summer, spectacular scenery and much better hotels. The outstanding natural beauty of the Carpathian Mountains and historic sites of the country are highly recommended.

The Open Doors group stayed for a few days at the Swan Hotel in Bucharest and visited three orphanages in the city as well as Ceauşescu's amazing palace. Almost all the visitors suffered stomach illnesses during the trip. This wasn't surprising because the hotel ran out of water and group members observed staff taking water from a fountain pool outside the building for guests to drink. The orphanages, which were the subject at that time of many television reports and documentary programmes in the West, were far more shocking when seen, heard and smelt first-hand by these visitors. One of the members of the group had a mild heart attack after visiting the worst of these places.

From Bucharest they went to Sibiu, Tirgu Mures, Sighisoara, Brasov and Poiana Brasov high in the mountains, which is a famous ski resort. They visited a Baptist church in Brasov and a Hungarian-speaking church in Sibiu. The two-week tour concluded back at the Savoy Hotel in Constanta.

One evening while they were there, Gabriel, their tour guide, asked them, "What would you like to do this evening?"

Their answer was, "We want to go to a church meeting."

The guide made a phone call (possibly to the local security police, who would know these things) to find out if there was a church meeting that night. The answer was that there were no meetings in Constanta that evening but there was one in a village not too far away, at the small Pentecostal church in Cumpăna, a village which at the time had a population of about ten thousand.

The group were pleased to have the chance to meet more local Christians before they returned home on 29th September and there was a buzz of excitement among them. The guide phoned ahead to tell the pastor that he was bringing a group of British visitors to their church.

This caused more excitement as the news soon spread among the church members around the village. That evening Cornel was sitting on a bench outside his house as many Romanians did, enjoying the cool of the early evening as the sun sank lower in the sky. He had been, in effect, discharged by the hospital and he did not know what the future held for him. As he sat, one of the village children passed and asked him if he was going to church, because foreign visitors were coming. He wanted to go, but it was a difficult and painful journey over poor roads on his crutches.

As he was contemplating what to do, his brother Gheorghe arrived in his green Trabant car to visit him. This was an unplanned visit and Cornel didn't know why he had come, except that he was nearby picking something up and decided to visit him and his parents while he was in the area.

Cornel asked him if he would take him to the church, and Gheorghe agreed. It wasn't a purpose-built church, but two rooms knocked into one to make a reasonable-sized meeting room. At the meeting, for Cornel and most of the congregation, this was their first contact with fellow Christians from the West. A translator was arranged so that the visitors could understand what was being said.

It is difficult for Christians in the West to appreciate just how much it meant for churches and believers in the communist countries to have contact with their fellow Christians in the West, and to know that they were praying for them. All through the years of restriction and persecution, it was some comfort to know that they were not alone. Their cry was always "Don't forget us!" This first contact with Western Christians was as source of joy and emotion for the congregation in Cumpăna.

Once the meeting had finished, there were many greetings, handshakes and hugs, accompanied by a lot of gestures and sign language. The visitors had brought with them a variety of small gifts to give to the church members, things that they thought might be appreciated, including soap, socks, toothbrushes, toothpaste, drawing books, pencils, sweets and clothing for the children. They distributed them after the meeting was concluded.

Tony and Pat Romano from Birmingham were members of the group of visitors. In the general hubbub after the meeting, they noticed Cornel standing on his crutches, leaning against the wall, as he had done throughout the meeting because he was unable to sit on the type of chairs in the room due to his ankylosing spondylitis. Tony and Pat approached him and offered some of the gifts, but he refused anything and told them that others in the room were in greater need of such things than he was. Because he knew all the families and spoke some English, he was able to point out those he knew were in the most need. Two things surprised Tony and Pat; firstly, that Cornel could speak enough English to converse with them and secondly his unselfishness in wanting the gifts to go to others. They were impressed by this and took his name and address to be able to write to him after returning home. His was one of a number of the church members' addresses that Tony and Pat had received on slips of paper written by some of the congregation.

Cornel was excited by the event, partly because he had never before met anyone from outside Romania and partly because he'd had his first chance to try out the English that he was learning on actual English people. Once the visitors were back in the bus, the ladies of the congregation joined hands and encircled the bus to sing a Romanian hymn as a way of saying farewell; it was very emotional. The thing that amazed the church most was that this group of British Christians had managed to come 2,500 kilometres and find them in such a small village which no one in the West had ever heard of.

Back home in Castle Vale, Birmingham, Tony and Pat belonged to a group of Christians who met regularly for prayer and fellowship. At their next meeting, they related the events of their trip and showed the rest of the group the slips of paper with the names and addresses. They decided to distribute the slips of paper by putting them into a hat and letting each member of the group pick one out. Cornel's address was drawn by David and Hilary, known to their friends as 'Dave and Hilly'. Pat and Tony emphasised the lack of food in any of the shops they had seen throughout their trip.

Dave and Hilly made up a food parcel and sent it to Cornel. Then, after some time, they received a letter back from Cornel (in English) thanking them. This began a long-term relationship and correspondence with him. They tried sending more parcels and small amounts of money, but this was very slow in both directions and some just never arrived. Dave and Hilly came to realise that God had called them to help Cornel in any way they could, especially as they became aware of the extent of his disability and the poverty his family had to endure. They were faithful to this calling and began to pray for him and to help him in various ways over many subsequent years.

In May 1991 John Miles decided to leave his job with Open Doors and was asked by the leaders of his church[4] to set up a church-based missions ministry. The name of the ministry was 'Riverside European and African Projects', or 'REAP' for short. The initial focus of the work was Eastern Europe, before later majoring in Africa. This meant many visits to friends and contacts around Romania. One of these visits was to the Pentecostal church in Constanta in the spring of 1991. When Tony and Pat (John's sister) heard that John and his wife Grace were going to Constanta, they asked if they would visit Cornel, which they agreed to do.

While in Constanta John mentioned Cornel to Pastor Nicu, and asked if they could visit him. Nicu knew of Cornel and the church in Cumpăna and he agreed to take them there. They met Cornel and his parents and saw the seemingly hopeless medical condition he was in. At the same time, they were impressed with his level of English. It was a brief visit with no opportunity to see the church or any of Cumpăna, but Cornel made an impression on them. They wondered how they could help him.

On another visit to the Pentecostal church in Constanta in the spring of 1992, which included another visit to Cornel, Cornel provided John and Grace with X-rays of his hips, which they brought back (and others were also posted) to show Mike Waldram, a friend in their church who was an orthopaedic surgeon working at The Royal Orthopaedic Hospital in Birmingham. Mike showed them to some colleagues at this specialist hospital to see if his condition could be helped.

The condition of Cornel's hip was very poor, and few surgeons would attempt to take on such a difficult task, even in this famous hospital. Alistair Sterling, a senior and very experienced surgeon thought he might be able to help Cornel, but felt that he would need to examine him first. Now Dave and Hilly took charge of the situation and it was arranged for Cornel to visit Birmingham for an examination of his hips.

In September 1992 Cornel and his brother Viorel came to Birmingham for two weeks. Dave and Hilly, together with Tony and Pat, met them at Gatwick airport and brought them to Birmingham, with Cornel travelling in Tony and Pat's Ford Fiesta and Viorel in Dave and

---

[4] Riverside Church, Birmingham, with a congregation of about five hundred attending at that time

Hilly's car. It wasn't easy for Cornel to get in and out of a small car, but his spine was sufficiently flexible at that time. Dave and Hilly accommodated them in their home in Castle Vale, Birmingham. They had recently moved from an apartment in a high-rise block to a three-bedroom house which was much easier for Cornel to access on his crutches.

An amusing memory of that first visit concerned the different sort of diet that Romanians have from our English one. Romanians eat large quantities of bread with all their meals, which Hilly didn't know. Viorel kept telling Cornel (in Romanian, of course) to ask for bread, but Cornel was too embarrassed and thought it would be impolite to ask. However, they had brought some sponge cake with them and they kept it hidden under their bed upstairs so that they could eat some to make up for the lack of bread. Years later, Cornel told Dave and Hilly about their secret food supply and the friends laughed about it together.

Mr Sterling's opinion was that he could best help Cornel by replacing his left hip, because the other hip had some movement but was restricted by the lack of movement in his left hip, preventing any bending of his torso. After the examination in Mr Sterling's private consulting rooms (which, of course, was extremely painful) testing how far the joints would move, a date for the surgery at the Royal Orthopaedic Hospital was set for June 1993. Cornel would need to be a private patient. This was only made possible because Mr Sterling and the anaesthetist generously offered to perform the operation free of charge. The only costs would be to the NHS for the time in the hospital bed, which turned out to be five weeks. Dave and Hilly undertook the task of raising the £3,000 for the NHS costs. In addition to them, among the contributors were a few who were in the original Open Doors tour party. Also, a relative of Dave and Hilly died at this time and left them some money (in the spring of 1993) which enabled them – in God's good timing – to raise the sum needed.

Cornel, now aged twenty-eight, arrived in June 1993, this time accompanied by his mother Maria. Dave and Hilly met them at Heathrow airport and provided accommodation for their visit, which lasted six weeks in all. The skill and experience of Mr Sterling resulted in a successful operation, and after the necessary period of recovery, Cornel was able to bend at the waist, enough to change his life completely. He was now able to sit at a table, sit almost normally in cars or aeroplanes, and do many things that had previously not been possible. During those weeks in hospital, Dave and Hilly, with Maria, visited Cornel every day.

This was quite a commitment because the hospital is located on the opposite side of Birmingham from their home, necessitating a round trip of about twenty-five miles through busy city traffic. In spite of the fact that Maria couldn't speak any English and Dave and Hilly had learned very little Romanian, they formed a warm bond together. Cornel's stay in the hospital was longer than normal for even such a difficult operation, but Mr Sterling, who saw him every day, wanted to make sure there was no infection and that he was as fit as possible to travel back to Romania. The air fares and other costs of these visits were beyond the abilities of Cornel and his family at that time. The local Christians responded to God's calling and the love of Christ in their hearts to meet all these costs.

Chapter Seven

Catalina's Story

CATALINA PENCIU, KNOWN TO EVERYONE AS 'CATI', CERtainly deserves a place under the heading 'Local Heroes', but her story is so amazing and unique that to do it justice, she needs her own chapter.

Catalina was born in Cumpăna on 20th December 1974, fifteen years before the fall of Ceauşescu and just over two years after Cornel moved there with his family, making their age difference nine years. Cornel says that he can even remember her birth. It was at a time when Cumpăna was much smaller. He was still able to run around the local streets and, like most small villages, everyone tended to know what was going on with everyone else, especially in the Christian community. In different ways, both Cornel and Cati faced enormous difficulties and suffering in their lives, but one thing is sure: God certainly had His plans for both of them.

To say that Cati's home life was difficult would be an understatement. It began with her parents splitting up before she was born. Her mother, Maria, then remarried after five years, but just three weeks into her marriage, the second husband, Mihai, was in a fight with another man and seriously injured him. He was sent to prison for five years for 'grievous bodily harm'. While Mihai was in prison, Cati's mother began building their own house in the Romanian rural way. They made their own blocks and Cati's grandparents, Ilie and Iona Banu, who lived nearby, helped. Cati and Maria moved in when just one room became habitable. This was a difficult time for Cati because she was often left alone in the house, even at night when her mother went to work. To pay for the construction materials, Maria worked long hours. Cati remembers it as a time when she was often afraid. The house had no electricity and the door could not be locked. Seven-year-old Cati cried a lot.

Maria waited the five years for her husband to return home. She visited him in prison at least once a month and took food. Cati was ten years old when her stepfather returned from prison and she expected that life would get better, but it didn't. It became much worse. He was an alcoholic and when he was drunk, he was very violent. He began drinking again and when he beat Maria, Cati would naturally and courageously try to protect her mother. The result was that she was beaten herself many times and lived in fear of this man.

Then Cati's mother became pregnant and had a baby boy. Because her mother worked so many hours, Cati often had to take care of the baby. It was very difficult for her. They had no proper nappies so she needed to improvise with pieces of cloth to try to keep the baby clean. The pieces of cloth had to be washed by hand and re-used many times. The family had two cows, a donkey, two pigs and lots of chickens. Cati always had to run to school because she was delayed with household responsibilities such as tending the animals. While she was there, her grandmother, who lived on the same street, came to care for the baby. Her grandmother was old and often came late, so Cati was then late for school, but the teachers knew about her difficult home situation and she was never punished for it.

Maria's marriage stumbled on with frequent break-ups and drunken violence. Sometimes Mihai just behaved irrationally and damaged the house and its contents. Windows were sometimes smashed and this was particularly difficult in the harsh Romanian winters. Somehow, he managed to keep his job as a welder in Constanta; it was in the evenings and at weekends that he was drunk. Four more babies were born (one of them died), increasing Cati's workload of caring for them and the household's animals. However, in spite of all this work and the violence, Cati determinedly continued to attend school as best she could.

Cati had an Aunt Silvia who lived just a hundred metres away and her aunt often helped her. She says that her Aunt Silvia loved her more that her own mother did. Cati's grandparents also lived nearby, and as she got older, she would increasingly run to their house to escape the violence and would stay there for a few weeks or months until things calmed down. With the arrival of more babies, Maria had to give up work to care for them.[5]

Mihai would beat Cati for seemingly no reason at all. She wasn't allowed to read books or have a light on when they eventually had electricity. He wouldn't let her go to church, which was only fifty metres away on the same street. Her mother had begun attending the church, but Cati was compelled to stay at home and do hard manual work outside the house. Once, when she said she couldn't do it, he tried to attack her with a pitchfork, but she was always alert and quick enough to run away. This incident seriously threatened her life, and she realised that it was becoming too dangerous for her to continue to live there. The neighbours could see what was happening and urged Cati to move and stay somewhere else, because she might not avoid serious injury or even death if she didn't.

Cati was now a beautiful young woman of sixteen. She lived with her grandparents for nine months but during that time her grandmother had a stroke and became bedridden. Cati helped her a lot, bathing and feeding her. They owned two cows and she milked them and made yoghurt and cheese. She even sold some of the milk in Constanta to provide much-needed money for the family. She was happy to do all this because while she was there, she could go to church, pray and spend time with God. This was the most important thing to her. Eventually, at the age of seventeen, reluctantly, she had to move back home to help her mother, and Aunt Silvia stepped in to help care for the grandmother. Cati then lived at home until she was twenty, running away to the grandparents' house whenever she needed to and usually returning after some weeks when things calmed down again, or when Maria and Mihai had one of their many separations.

Through all this, Cati held on tenaciously to her faith in God, even though her life was so difficult. It was God alone who loved her unconditionally. God saw all her tears and she knew she had to cling on to this foundation in her life. It was at this time that she was baptised by the local Pentecostal church where she worshiped. The baptism took place outside the village in a small canal. Her mother was also baptised at the same service. Maria had been attending the church for some years. Cornel, of course, was the photographer on hand to record the happy occasion. Baptism is supposed to mark a spiritual transition to a new

---

[5] Cati has four surviving siblings: two half-brothers and two half-sisters.

relationship with God and a transformation in the life of the believer. Sadly, future events cast a serious doubt about the effect this had in Maria's life.

Cati's first real contact with Cornel had been when she was just thirteen. Cornel had taken Maria's photograph for the ID card and Cati was sent to collect it from his house. Cornel was sitting on a bench outside the house and they had a short conversation. Maria happened to see Cati as she was just leaving, and became very angry because in the Romanian culture at that time it was not acceptable for a girl even to talk briefly with a handicapped man. When Cati arrived back home, her mother beat her very severely with a heavy steel coat hanger, leaving her with many bruises on her arms and legs. Handicapped people suffered extreme prejudice, and Maria, being a very proud woman, didn't want a daughter of hers to be seen talking to a handicapped man. But this only partially explains her violent reaction to a simple, innocent conversation.

The next day Maria sent Cati to the doctor with one of her younger siblings and the doctor observed that Cati wasn't well. She asked her what was wrong, but Cati wouldn't tell the doctor what had happened.[6] The beating was an insane reaction, but also an early indication of what Cati would eventually need to suffer for her association with Cornel.

During her late teens Cati's contact with Cornel was in the context of their church. She was a member of the youth and they sometimes went to Cornel's house for group photos. There was no particular friendship between them. They were just aware of each other as members of the same church. All the church members knew of Cornel's visit to the United Kingdom in September 1992 and his subsequent surgery in June 1993. But few of them realised the extent of the change in his physical condition and the improvement that it meant for his future. For Cornel, everything was different. Apart from the obvious physical improvement, a radical change in his thinking and self-confidence had taken place. He was amazed at how differently handicapped people were regarded in Britain, where they were given respect and special facilities in public places. No one stared at them in public. He says that in Romanian culture handicapped people were despised and almost regarded as sub-human. More recently, attitudes have been changing as the population has been exposed – through travel, media and the Internet – to other cultures and attitudes.

---

[6] Cornel only heard about this from Cati about seven years later.

Now Cornel began to wonder if, perhaps, with his improved physical state, one day he could marry. His mother prayed fervently every night for him. He often overheard her prayers. She awoke and prayed every night at 02.00 am. She was getting older and was increasingly concerned about who would care for him once she became too old or died. However, he still couldn't see himself asking anyone to marry him. This was mentally a very low time for Cornel. He was lonely and depressed as he thought about his future. He would like to be married but couldn't see any way for this to happen. One thing he resolved, and said to God in his prayers, was that if he were to get married, it would have to be the girl asking or proposing to him – the opposite of the normal custom. It was asking a lot but for him, he could not accept anything else – not in Romania in those days.

When Cati was twenty she decided to leave home and live with her Godmother in Constanta, who knew about her desperate situation and had offered her accommodation. Materially it would have been a good move for Cati and a chance to begin a new life, find a job and make new friends away from the problems she faced at home. In Romanian culture Godparents have a more significant caring role than in the West, especially for Christians. But her Godparents were not Christians and it would mean moving from her church and Christian friends in Cumpăna. Nevertheless, her circumstances at home were so bad that she was prepared to go.

On the day that she planned to leave her home, she awoke to find that her right knee was swollen and very painful. There was no apparent cause for this. It had never given her a problem before. It was so bad that she couldn't walk. This meant that instead of going to Constanta, she was admitted to hospital with her knee problem. Looking back, she realises that through this strange episode, God was stopping her from moving away. She was bedridden for three weeks. It was a new experience for her, not being able to walk or even get to the toilet. As she lay in hospital, she began to think about Cornel and wonder what it must be like for him to be in a similar position, but in his case, permanently. The doctors were considering the need for an operation on her knee, which she really did not want. Other patients in the hospital were urging her not to have it because they had seen that other patients seemed to be in a worse condition after the operation than before having it. Cati fasted for a day and prayed, telling God that if He helped her to recover without an operation, when she returned home she would begin visiting Cornel just as an act of kindness. (She had no romantic attachment to Cornel, just a feeling of sympathy for someone in his position, having had a similar, though much shorter, experience herself.) As soon as she prayed that prayer, her knee quickly recovered and she was discharged from the hospital.

Cati had some dreams which she much later recognised as God speaking to her. When she was just eighteen, she fasted for three days and prayed about her future. Her life was so difficult that she longed to get married to someone and be able to live a better life. She had no one in mind to marry, but she hoped that one day this would happen. She was an attractive young woman who would have no difficulty in finding a husband. Then she had a dream in which someone spoke to her and asked her if she really wanted to know about her future husband. She said that she did want to know. The person said that all he could tell her was that her husband would have a health problem. Later, when she was still living with her grandparents and just before her knee problem, she had another dream. In it she was walking down a street and saw a shop that sold perfume. In the shop a man was buying some very expensive perfume for his wife. Cati said that she could never afford such expensive perfume. Cornel was also in the shop when she entered. He overheard Cati saying this and he said to her, "I could buy you that perfume."

Cornel had also received dreams. When he was twenty-five he had a vivid dream in which he was married and had children. Cornel thought about this dream and asked God for confirmation that if it was from Him, he would have the dream again. Some weeks later he had exactly the same dream again. Before this he hardly dared to think about such a possibility. He had resigned himself to a single life. Who would ever want to marry a person with such a handicap such as his, especially in the prevailing culture in which he lived?

Both Cornel and Cati, when they had these dreams, had no idea how or when such events could possibly happen, and certainly didn't think of any particular person. They just kept the dreams at the back of their minds and didn't tell anyone about them. Dreams can be strange, but in the Bible there are many occasions when God spoke to individuals through dreams and we should never dismiss the possibility that God wants so speak to us in this way.

The first time Cati visited Cornel at his home was after she came out of the hospital and, surprisingly, it was with her mother's permission. This was in contrast to Maria's violent reaction when Cati was thirteen. The reason for this change of attitude was that Cati's mother and Cornel's sister, also named Maria, had been in hospital at the same time for childbirth and they had become good friends. Cornel's sister and her husband Mircea also lived in Cumpăna, about a kilometre from Cornel's house. Cornel's sister gave birth to a daughter named Roxana and Cati's mother gave birth to a son named Emanuel. The two Marias had light-heartedly speculated that perhaps in the future Emanuel might marry Roxana.

Cati explained to her mother that she had promised God that she would visit Cornel as an act of kindness, and she was allowed to go. It was customary to take some small gift such as chocolate or yoghurt when you visited someone who was sick, so whenever Cati visited she took such a gift. Cati increasingly found that she wanted to visit Cornel. They were becoming friends and Cati enjoyed having someone to talk to who was intelligent, treated her with respect and took her seriously.

Cati volunteered to clean the church on Sunday afternoons between morning and afternoon services. This was a time of the week when she was away from the control of her mother and she visited Cornel covertly for about twenty minutes, once or twice a month. During these visits they became closer in their friendship and she felt confident enough to tell Cornel – often with tears – about her life, with the difficulties and violence she had endured. There was a shared empathy between them. They had both suffered difficult lives, albeit in different ways.

CHAPTER EIGHT

Triumph Over Opposition

IT WAS JUST ONE DAY AFTER CATI HAD RETURNED HOME from the hospital following her knee problem, and Cornel was feeling particularly low. He asked God to show him the reason for the frustration and depression he was feeling. It was a desperate prayer. As he finished praying, there was a knock on the door and to his surprise it was Cati, on the first of her visits to him after she had been discharged from hospital. Cornel dismissed this as a coincidence. Many girls came to his house to have their pictures taken and Cati was just one of those. Then on another day, as he was praying a similar prayer, there was another knock at the door and Cati was there again. God is gracious enough that if we don't get the message first time, He will repeat it. Even though he could see that somehow God had spoken to him, he didn't know what it meant or how things would turn out. Thus began a series of visits from Cati and their friendship deepened.

Cati felt guilty about covertly visiting Cornel because it was against the culture for a girl to visit a boy. Of course, it was normally the other way round, but still she wanted to go. Although she knew that Cornel would not be allowed to visit her, she continued the visits because it was the only way they could see each other. Although Maria didn't know about Cati's visits, Cornel's neighbours could see her coming and going. Cornel shared the house with his parents, but he had a different entrance leading to his own room. This was necessary for his photography business. Cati was conflicted in her mind about the visits, so she asked God if it was right for her to continue.

The answer came in a church prayer meeting with a visiting prophet from Mangalia, which is about forty kilometres away. He didn't know Cati or any of her circumstances, but during the meeting, as everyone was praying, he came to Cati with a prophetic word. He simply said, "This word is for you: God appreciates that you asked Him about this; continue to go there." Cati was amazed that God would answer her in such a direct way, and through a prophet that didn't even know her. There was nothing about marriage or a relationship, just the one simple message that she needed to hear. The message was powerful in its bare simplicity. This gave her the courage to continue with her visits, knowing that if no one else approved, God did, and that is what mattered most to her.

It was during these visits in 1995 that both Cati and Cornel began to realise that they were attracted to each other, but they were afraid to bring up the subject for discussion. One of Cati's friends had attempted some matchmaking and introduced her to a young man her own age, suggesting that they should develop their relationship. He was a fine young man but Cati just didn't like him and that was the end of the matter. Cornel still knew that he could not be the one to initiate any conversation about marriage. He was afraid that if he did bring up the subject he would offend or hurt Cati, and so he kept quiet. It was just asking too much of any young attractive girl to take on such a marriage to a man with his level of disability. Even with his improved condition he knew that he would never go out to work and support a family as other husbands did or be able to play football with a son if God gave him one. No; it was too much and still seemed like a far-fetched dream. He knew that he could never ask any girl to marry him, and that was that! Any such idea or proposal would have to come from the girl and he couldn't imagine that happening.

Cati realised that, in spite of their mutual attraction, Cornel was never going to ask her to marry him and she understood why. Her family had found out that she was visiting Cornel and warned her to stop. This was bringing things to a head and Cati realised that she needed to take the initiative and she needed to do so immediately. On her next visit, in October 1995, two years and three months after Cornel's surgery in England and two months before her twentieth birthday, she decided that she would break the silence on this matter, and it was going to take courage. At first, she just asked Cornel if he thought that he would ever get married. He was shocked that she had brought up the subject, but his answer was yes.

Cati then followed up this question with another question that Cornel had thought he would never hear: "Will you marry me?" This was totally against the culture, but it was the breakthrough that they both needed. They were very aware that severe difficulties now faced Cati when she told her family and she was going to need great courage. Cornel and Cati made an agreement that if she ever changed her mind because of the pressure they knew she would come under, she would tell him immediately. He told her that their life together would be difficult and that he had no money, only forty dollars. She said she didn't care about money, all she wanted was Cornel. Cati's mother naturally wanted her daughter to marry, but to anyone except him!

When, in January 1996, Cati told her mother that she was going to marry Cornel, her reaction was furious and violent. There now began a family effort to force Cati to change her mind. She was beaten every day and was not allowed out to see Cornel. Her mother stopped feeding her properly and kept her clothes from her. Later, Cati moved to live for four weeks with her Aunt Martha, who lived about half a kilometre away, to escape the violence. Aunt Martha was about to give birth to her thirteenth child and Cati could help her with cooking and other family chores. Later she moved to stay with her Aunt Oprica. Her mother even came there to beat her. She accused her of having an immoral relationship with Cornel and suggested that she was pregnant or that he had given her drugs. Of course, none of this was true. Her mother even wanted to take her to the doctor to prove she was a virgin.

Later that month the whole family gathered to put pressure on Cati to change her mind. They threatened to lock her in the basement for five years. Her response was that even if they did that, she would not change her mind. They suggested one or two boys that she might marry. With this they tried to bribe her with promises to give her the grandfather's house and money, but she remained resolute that she would marry Cornel. She told them plainly, "My heart belongs to Cornel." Her family's response was that she could not live at home any longer. Her grandfather offered to accommodate her and keep an eye on her.

One night she was being badly beaten by four family members together. She ran out of the house to escape. She was only dressed in T-shirt and tights but she grabbed a coat and ran out into the snow in bare feet. A cousin chased after her and caught her. As she was being held, another cousin came and took over from the first one and said that he would take care of the situation. But he was sympathetic and he let her go, so she ran to her Aunt Oprica's house. Oprica had a daughter the same size as Cati and she provided her with some of her daughter's clothes. After this awful incident she went to stay again at her grandfather's house.

Apart from Cornel's family, virtually everyone, including some of the members of the church, were against this marriage. Both Cornel and Cati were under enormous pressure from so many sides, but they never gave up; they didn't even think of doing so. Two people, who had suffered so much pain and ill-treatment in their lives, albeit in very different ways, and had clung on to the love of God, now saw a future together and nothing was going to stop them. Their faith in God had laid a strong spiritual foundation in their lives, but there is no doubt that the things they had suffered had also made them tough! In Africa there is a saying, 'What doesn't kill us makes us stronger.' This truth can certainly be applied to Cornel and Cati. Now they began to secretly make their marriage plans.

It was not until late March 1996 that Cati – now back living with her grandparents – told her grandfather that she was going to get married in two weeks, so he could never say she hadn't told him. They wanted to get married in their own church, but they knew that there would be pressure against this from Cati's family and many of the church members. To put pressure back on the church to allow them to have a church wedding ceremony, they decided to first have a civil wedding in Constanta at the government Registry Office, but to tell no one about their plans. Although they would be legally married, they agreed together that they would not consider themselves married until after their church wedding, if they could persuade the church, and particularly the pastor, to perform the ceremony.

Cornel's mother, Maria, was pleased that they wanted to marry. For her it was an answer to all those prayers she had so earnestly prayed in the middle of the night; but at the same time, she was fearful of the church and of a family war she thought it might stir up. Cornel knew that they were going to need some help, such as with transport. One day his brother Gheorghe, who had a car, came to visit. He was the first family member apart from his mother that Cornel told about the plan to marry. In Romania you couldn't get married without first getting a blood test, a medical certificate and other paperwork. Then there had to be a ten-day wait. Gheorghe helped and took them to Constanta to get all the necessary formalities completed. If they had done this in Cumpăna, the news would have quickly spread to everyone in the village and this would have stirred up the opposition and made things even more difficult.

After the paperwork was completed, and before Cati told her grandfather, some of her family came to see Cornel and told him that Cati had changed her mind and given up on him. They said she was mentally ill. He of course knew that these things were not true. If she did change her mind, he would be the first one she would tell. Cornel just told them that he didn't believe them and that he and Cati were definitely getting married. This feeble attempt to stop the marriage by deception failed, just as the beatings and bad treatment had also failed. To Cati they made pessimistic predictions: "You are going to have a hard life with this man. You are a fool to continue with this plan." Throughout all this opposition, both Cornel and Cati kept a calm disposition, answering everything without being argumentative or showing anger. Cati tried to reason with her mother by reminding her that she had waited five years for her husband Mihai when he was in prison and that she had remained faithful to him, taking him food (at times even taking Cati's food for him) even though she knew he was an alcoholic.

Finally, the day came on 8th April 1996. With all the paperwork completed, Gheorghe arrived first at Cornel's house in his Trabant (probably the worst car ever manufactured and made partly of compressed cardboard). Maria had ironed her son's clothes and he had borrowed a suit from Gheorghe. She prayed for him, blessed him and off they drove to pick up Cati to go to the Registry office in Constanta. It was pouring with rain and on the way the 'Trabbie' – true to form – broke down. This caused some panic because if they missed the allotted time slot at the Registry Office, they would need to start all over again. The 'Trabbie' was soon fixed and they arrived in time for their appointment with the Registrar, and were legally married in a civil ceremony. The day before the civil ceremony they told Cornel's brother Viorel about the wedding and he also came to the ceremony.

Now the next task was to convince the church to get involved. From the Registry Office they first went to the home of Pastor Nicu Man, one of the associate pastors of the main Pentecostal church in Constanta. He already knew part of their story, but they explained the whole situation to him. They were encouraged by this pastor and he told them that they had done the right thing in coming first to him for advice. It was a Monday and that evening there was a regular church leaders' meeting. He suggested that they attend it and explain to the leaders their situation. It was important at this stage that Cornel and Cati stayed in separate places. Cati went to Gheorghe's house where she would live until their

Christian marriage ceremony could be completed, and then he drove Cornel home to Cumpăna. In the evening, Gheorghe collected Cornel again and took them both to the leaders' meeting in Constanta. Later, Gheorghe took Cati to his house and Viorel took Cornel back to his parents' house.

Sadly, the senior pastor of the Constanta church was very critical of what they had done and was the main voice of opposition. But Pastor Nicu Man argued convincingly that Cornel and Cati had done the right thing and acted righteously. They had not had any sexual contact and didn't intend to until a Christian ceremony was performed.

The discussion was going nowhere. Pastor Nicu Man wisely suggested that they should pray together to seek God's will. He prayed prayer after prayer and, as he continued to pray, everything calmed down and a more reasonable discussion followed. The leadership reached the conclusion that Cornel and Cati had done the righteous thing in not sleeping together, even though they were entitled to do so, and that there was nothing in the Bible to indicate that they had sinned in any way, which of course was true.

The date of 21st April was set for their wedding ceremony, thirteen days later, in Cumpăna at Cornel's house. They didn't want it to be in the church because too many of the members were against their marriage and as it would then be a public ceremony, if it were held in the church then anyone in the village could turn up. The risk of a disrupted ceremony was just too great. During those intervening days Cati stayed in Constanta with Gheorghe's family and she and Cornel didn't see each other until their wedding day. Cati's family had lined up several young men who would have willingly married her, but she wasn't interested and they were not even Christians. Cornel suspects that these potential suitors were also offered incentives of money and a house.

A few days before the church ceremony, Cati's mother came to Cornel and demanded to know where her daughter was. Cornel had their legal wedding certificate and pointed out that Cati was legally his wife. Later that night Cati's mother went to the home of the Chief of Police (not the police station) and complained that Cornel had stolen her daughter and said that she wanted her back. The Police Chief, Cornel Nazare, had been friends with Cornel for a long time and he wasn't prepared to give any credence to false accusations. He had often brought criminals whom he had arrested to Cornel to have their photos taken. He simply asked Maria how old Cati was. Maria had to admit that she was twenty-one. This ended the discussion; Cati was legally of an age to make her own choices. The Police Chief just sent her home. Pastor Man went to the church in Cumpăna to try to reconcile Maria with Cornel and Cati, but to no avail.

During the wedding service Cati's mother stood about thirty metres away, angry and frustrated. She had been invited to attend, but she had refused to accept. Other church members stood near, but they were intimidated by Maria's fierce anger and kept their distance. She saw these people every Sunday in church and they didn't want to be disloyal to one of their members, even though they didn't consider her to live a Christian lifestyle. What kind of Christian beats her daughter in the way she had?

Only about forty invited guests were allowed to attend. This included all of Cornel's family; Pastor Man, who conducted the ceremony, and his wife; Pastor Zegrea and his wife from the Constanta church; Nicu Zaraf, the leader of the church in Cumpăna; some of Cati's family; and some of the young Christians from the Cumpăna church. Apart from Pastor Man, the other pastor also spoke during the wedding. Some men were posted at the door who would allow only the invited guests in. Only if Cati's mother came in peace would she be allowed in. Cati's abusive stepfather, Mihai, just stayed at home.

It was a simple ceremony, but with all the normal ceremonial content. There were no rings as the church in Cumpăna didn't approve of them. After the wedding a meal was provided for the guests and the atmosphere was one of rejoicing, as it should be at a wedding; especially one which enjoyed God's approval and blessing.

Chapter Nine

The In-Between Years

AFTER THEIR CHRISTIAN WEDDING ON APRIL 21ST 1996, Cornel and Cati could reflect that they had, by the grace of God, overcome barriers that would simply crush the spirit of most people. After years of suffering and pain, God had enveloped them in His love – which had always been there and was now manifested in the happiness they shared as a married couple. There were more challenges to come, such as health issues for Cornel and financial uncertainty, but facing them together would be easier. They were a boy and a girl who had grown up in a small, almost unknown village in eastern Romania, just seven kilometres from The Black Sea, but God knew all about them and the dreams that they hardly dared to acknowledge. God heard and answered their prayers and their dreams had become reality.

They lived with Cornel's parents, and as they contemplated the immediate future, at the top of their agenda was reconciliation with Cati's family. This was something they very much wished for and they were prepared to make the first moves. About two weeks after their wedding Cati saw her grandfather and asked him to try to facilitate reconciliation in the family. She pointed out the obvious fact that they were now married and nothing would change that, so why not try to use his considerable influence and talk to Cati's mother, because it was better for everyone that they lived in peace. He was willing to do this, and he went and talked to his daughter Maria. The result was that near the end of May 1996, about five weeks after their marriage, Cati went to her mother's house for a meeting with her mother and her grandfather.

Bearing in mind Cornel's very limited mobility, it was clear that he and Cati were going to need their own car if they were going to get around as a couple, and eventually as a family if the Lord granted them the blessing of children. Fortunately, there was one available. They had been given money from guests at their wedding, which is a Romanian custom, and Cornel's mother also helped them as much as she could. This enabled them to buy a ten-year-old yellow Dacia 1300 car for about £1,000 from Viorel, Cornel's brother, who was going to Germany to work for a while. The Dacia Company had acquired the tooling and basic designs of the Renault 12, a medium-sized family car, and began producing it in Romania in August 1969. It was not very reliable and the engines didn't last long. The one big advantage it had was that it was easy to work on and the Romanian do-it-yourself culture meant that there was an amateur mechanic on every corner and in every family!

Cati was a quick learner. She began by driving the car around the village and the surrounding fields. Then she took a few lessons and successfully passed the driving test on December 12th in that very eventful year. Learning to drive meant that Cati was able to drive in her own car to the meeting with her mother. Cornel went with her and stayed in the car, waiting to see what the outcome would be.

Maria wanted the neighbours to see that Cati had first come to her house to ask for reconciliation. It was a matter of pride. Cati didn't mind this though, and arriving in her own car gave her something to be proud about herself. Naturally, Cati was fearful of going into the house because it held so many violent and traumatic memories for her, so the meeting was outside and they just stood in the sunshine and talked for a while. Looking back, Cornel jokes that standing made it easier to run away!

The atmosphere at the meeting was fine and Maria assured Cati that she had no reason to fear her anymore. Cati invited them to come to the home of Cornel's parents for a family meal to cement the reconciliation, so the two families gathered together for the meal. This time the atmosphere was very cordial, and Maria even began to show some remorse for the way she had treated Cati. Cati's stepfather Mihai did not attend. He was busy fighting his own demons and trying to hold down a job whilst being an alcoholic. Cati (still officially a learner driver) fetched her grandparents in her car because her grandmother was frail after her stroke. Cati had been very close to her aunt Sylvia who had recently died, so she invited Sylvia's oldest son to represent that branch of the family. Before the wedding Maria told everyone how much she hated Cornel and Cati, but now she promised to stop saying things like that and said that she would explain to everyone that the feud was over. It should be remembered that many of the people, from both sides at this gathering, not only lived in the same small village and had many relatives in common, but also attended the same church. This was another powerful motive for them to try to forget the past and live in peace with each other as best they could. After this Cornel and Cati resumed regular attendance at their Pentecostal church.

Cornel and Cati had originally planned to marry in the autumn, but they decided to bring the date forward because things were getting so difficult for Cati. It had been planned for Cornel to return to Britain with his brother Gheorghe in August the same year so that he could see his surgeon for a follow up check on his hip and spend some time with his friends in England. Details about the trip were discussed in February with a phone call to Dave and Hilly in Castle Vale. International communications at this time were not easy. Letters took weeks and the time to organise things which required questions, replies and follow-up letters took months. Very few people in rural Romania had their own phones at that time. This meant that Cornel had to go into Constanta to access a landline to make international calls to Dave and Hilly. When he called them to finally tie up the arrangements for the visit, they asked him who would be accompanying him. To their astonishment, his answer was, "My future wife." Dave and Hilly had not heard about the upcoming marriage because of the communication difficulties. Needless to say, they were delighted.

The trip was then arranged and in August 1996 Cornel and Cati flew to England for a five-week holiday, staying – of course – with Dave and Hilly, who facilitated the trip. Apart from the follow-up examination with Cornel's surgeon, Alistair Sterling, they also wanted some advice on the possibility of Cornel's ankylosing spondylitis being hereditary. Some of the doctors Cornel had seen suggested that his condition might be passed on to any children that they might have. Dr Ann Griffiths was a Christian GP who lived in the Castle Vale estate, so they went to see her. She in turn sought the advice of a specialist geneticist, who told her that it was very unlikely that their children would develop AS. This put their minds at rest and, as events turned out, it was probably during this holiday that their first child was conceived.

Once they returned home to Cumpăna it soon became obvious that Cati was pregnant and the following year, on June 3rd 1997, Cati gave birth to a healthy and beautiful baby girl. They called her Camelia and she became known to everyone simply as 'Cami'. She was born in the hospital in Constanta. In those days in Romania husbands were not allowed to attend the birth of their children, and when Cati went into labour Cornel's brother Viorel took her to the hospital; it was quicker than waiting for an ambulance. Cornel just had to sit and wait anxiously for any news of mother and baby because they had no phone. Did the delivery go well? Were Cati and the baby all right? Was it a boy or a girl? It was ten thirty that evening before he finally heard the answers to these questions, and the news was all good.

Cornel resumed his photography business and was regarded as the best of the three photographers working in Cumpăna, even though he had never been trained for it. Everything was self-taught, including the developing of the prints in colour. One effect of the 1989 revolution was that many more people could travel abroad and wanted passport photographs. This, in addition to the ID cards, the police work, baptisms and weddings, meant a steady, if modest, income for the family. Cati and Cornel's mother supplemented the income with produce from their land, the cows and chickens.

Inevitably their thoughts now turned to building their own house and, of course, building it in the usual Romanian do-it-yourself way. It was August 1997 and the first need was for a plot of land. After the revolution the ownership of land became confused and uncertain. All the land now theoretically belonged to the local authorities, but with the new-found freedom, many people wanted to build themselves a house. There were many plots of land that did not belong to anyone with a hereditary title to them. Some people just went and staked out a plot and declared that it was now available for them to build on; the legal paperwork for the land was usually sorted out afterwards. Before her death, Cati's aunt Sylvia had been bold enough to secure two plots of land on the edge of Cumpăna. She gave one of the plots to Cati (before they were married), which measured seven hundred square metres.

Their plan was to just build a small bungalow with a living room, one bedroom and a bathroom. Sometime later they added two more rooms and a hallway which gave access to all the other rooms. This way they were able to spread the cost, which enabled them to move in much sooner. Cornel's father and a group of friends and relatives, including Cornel's nephews and Cati's cousins, swung into action. They dug trenches, fetched rocks for hardcore to fill them and then topped them off with about half a metre of concrete to complete the foundations. There was a plentiful supply of rocks from the nearby excavations of the 'Danube to Black Sea' canal which was still under construction. It was back-breaking work wielding sledgehammers under the hot summer sun, but Romanians are not afraid of hard work! Then came the making of the blocks for the main construction; again, organised by Cornel's father.

Once the blocks were dried, the same yellow clay that the blocks were made from was used as cement. This alone would not be a very strong structure, except that the walls inside and out were then strengthened with wire mesh attached with nails to the walls. The mesh then acted as a strong anchoring system for the plastering. They made their own plaster by mixing sand, cement and lime. Once everything was finished and dried, it was a strong structure built at a fraction of the cost a construction company would charge. By November 1997 the walls were built and the roof was on, but as yet there were no doors or windows. After a break for the severe winter weather, they began plastering the walls inside and out. In May 1998, two years after they were married, Cornel and Cati were able to move into their own home.

As Cornel's parents aged, Maria wanted to be closer to Cornel and Cati's house and of course to her lovely granddaughter. With the help of Viorel and Gheorghe they sold their own house, purchased a plot and built another just thirty-six metres from Cornel and Cati's place on 'Dimitrie Cantemir' Street. This made it easier for Maria to walk between the two properties, especially in the winter. With the cash from their house sale they didn't need to make their own blocks but were able to buy them and put in strong concrete foundations.

Eventually, the government decided on a system of payment for these plots of land. The local government auctioned leases for each plot, and Cornel and Cati successfully bid for their plot. Payment was in the form of a forty-nine-year lease, for which they paid an amount each year. The disadvantage was that the local government kept raising the payment every year. The only sensible option was to purchase the plot outright. They saved their money, borrowed some from the bank, and with help from friends in Britain, were able to pay the asking price of $4,300 in two instalments – and completed in March 2007. Finally, after eleven years of marriage, they owned their own plot of land and the house that they had built on it. Another source of income was from Cati and Cornel's six nephews, who were able to make a lot of extra blocks and sell them. The materials were free and so was the labour, resulting in a one hundred percent profit.

In spite of all the predictions of doom and gloom about their marriage, which had fed the village gossip grapevine, and in spite of all the prejudice, opposition and scorn that they had initially endured during the course of the early months and years of their marriage, they had achieved a family reconciliation, acquired a car, enjoyed a foreign holiday in England, experienced the birth of a lovely baby girl and moved into their own house. Things were turning out very well indeed! God was demonstrating His love and grace to Cornel and Cati in a very practical way. Their faith, courage and persistence had been rewarded. God was also showing what He thought about the disdain and bad treatment of those with any kind of handicap. Cornel's visits to Britain for medical treatment had opened his eyes to the fact that there existed in other parts of Europe a completely different and superior attitude towards, provision for and acceptance of disability. Nowadays Romania is changing and the treatment of orphans, the disabled, widows and the destitute is improving as the years pass. Changes that took over two hundred years in the West are coming about much quicker in Romania now that communist attitudes to what they considered as 'non-productive' elements of the population are draining away.

Land Reform

During the communist era most of the rural land which was originally privately owned was confiscated by the state, and a system of 'collectives' was imposed and farmed by rural workers. The post-revolution government initially resisted calls to break up the collective system, but the overwhelming public and political opposition and pressure successfully led to restitution of the land to its former owners. Most families had kept their title deeds and passed them down to their children and grandchildren. Rural workers without land were to be given plots to own. Before the revolution, 411 state farms and 3,776 cooperatives accounted for almost all the country's arable land. In 1991 about 65% of the land belonging to cooperatives was restored to former owners or their descendants. About 3.7 million rural households repossessed land, deciding to farm it either individually or in associations. By 2004 the land privatisation process was largely complete.

By the grace of God and through the love of friends and family, Cornel and Cati's lives had taken a dramatic turn for the better, but there were still challenges. Ankylosing spondylitis is incurable and progressive and, as we have seen, Cornel's condition had not been diagnosed in his childhood and it was only at the late age of eighteen that his true condition was revealed. There are a number of 'what ifs'. What if he had been diagnosed at the age of thirteen? What if he'd had access to the best treatment? Wouldn't his condition be so much better? From a human perspective this is certainly true, but Cornel and Cati clung on to the Christian principle that God is ultimately in control and has a plan for each of us. In the life of Job in the Bible we can see his righteous response to the horrific events that befell him: "Shall we indeed accept good from God, and shall we not accept adversity?"[7]

On the positive side, the skill of orthopaedic surgeon Alistair Sterling had transformed Cornel's life, and in the years following the surgery, the more appropriate medication also helped. Obtaining the medication in Romania was very difficult at that time. Cornel needed expensive steroids twice a year for ten days at a time. The state gave some help with the costs, but he had to find the majority of the money. The steroids would take the pain away for a while, but it always came back. Cornel also needed blood tests once, and sometimes twice, a month. He was only entitled to one free blood test each year from the state, so most of the treatments and blood tests needed to be done privately and had to be paid for. The costs of the tests were between £30 and £100 per month, depending on how many there were and what the tests were for. The medication was often difficult to find for weeks and they needed to visit lots of pharmacies searching for it. Without their Dacia car it would have been almost impossible. The total cost of the medication and the blood tests could often amount to £200 a month. To obtain these from the Romanian health service just wasn't practical. Appointments took weeks and sometimes months to come through. The state doctors also had to be paid in the form of a bribe before they would do anything. Without the continuing help from their Christian friends in England, none of this would have been possible. It is not an exaggeration to say that for Cornel this was life-saving.

During these years Cornel went to Bucharest several times and stayed in hospital for a month to try different medications and physiotherapy. None of it helped even though the doctors and therapists were doing their best; his condition was too advanced for the treatment to have any real effect. He also began to have pain from his gallbladder. He was supposed to have an operation for this to be removed, but the surgeon who was

---

[7] Job 2:10

ready to do the operation was unable to find an anaesthetist willing or able to be involved, because Cornel's airway was too constricted due to his ankylosing spondylitis. Fortunately, the gallbladder problem cleared up without surgery. A further complication arose in the form of Hepatitis 'C' which was diagnosed in June 2009. He probably contracted this from infected blood given him by transfusion in one the operations he had gone through, or possibly through being given an injection from a syringe that had been used more than once. He will never know for sure, but the course of treatment for this had very bad side-effects. After the first injection the reaction was so severe that Cati was afraid that he might die. At his lowest point Cornel was so weak that he couldn't feed himself or go to the toilet without help. The further treatment was less traumatic but still difficult. He was told that only about 35% of patients completed this course of treatment; the others gave up because of the side-effects. It took a year before Cornel fully recovered.

In spite of Cornel's litany of health problems, side-effects of various medications and the slow but undeniable progression of his ankylosing spondylitis, Cornel and Cati were still hopeful of enlarging their family. In March 2007 Cati had a miscarriage, which is disappointing to any couple who are hoping for another child. The disappointment didn't last too long, though, because on March 20th 2008 their second daughter, Hilary-Gabriela, was born. She was, of course, named after their English friend Hilly. Cami now had a baby sister, ten years her junior.

CHAPTER TEN

God Still at Work

THE STRONG FOUNDATIONS THAT UNDERGIRDED THE NEW home in which Maria lived her final years are perhaps a fitting metaphor for the godly way she lived her life and served the God she loved. Not only was her own life built on strong foundations, but she was able to cement them into the lives of her children. As the scripture powerfully tells Christians in 1 Corinthians 3:11, '...no one can lay any foundation other than the one already laid, which is Jesus Christ.'

Cornel's mother died in October 2002, aged seventy-two. Maria was a faithful, strong Christian influence by word and example which profoundly influenced Cornel's life. Only eternity will reveal the full effect of her constant prayers for him and the rest of her family. Her faith in Christ was her strength and the measure by which she made her decisions. She had worked hard all her life and she was constantly with Cornel to help him, especially through the darkest days of extreme pain and immobility.

Her full reward, of course, will be in heaven, but in her latter years there was also joy. She had travelled to Britain with Cornel for his hip surgery and witnessed first-hand the life-changing difference this had made to her son in the following months. In perhaps the most surprising answer to her years of prayer for Cornel, he had married the beautiful Cati, seven years before Maria's death. This relieved her greatest anxiety: who would care for Cornel after she had gone? She even had the delight of a lovely granddaughter, Cami, who was aged five when Maria died.

The day before her death, Cornel and Cati went to visit her. They could see that her condition had deteriorated, but they never thought that she was about to die. Later, at about 8.00 pm, Cati went to give her an injection and Maria said to Cati, "I will pass away this night; please take care of Cornel." She died that night at about 2.00 am. She had walked all her life with the Lord and He had shown her that the time had finally come for her to come home to Him. No more pain, no more hard work, no more cares, only joy.

Her husband Gheorghe died in February 2014 aged eighty, having outlived Maria by twelve years. He had also outlived Romania's communist era and lived through some of his country's most difficult years. He was a hard worker and a champion of the Romanian do-it-yourself culture.

If we search the Scriptures for examples of God's calling on the lives of His servants, it becomes obvious that the callings and ministries that come from Him are almost always long-term. 'For the gifts and the calling of God are irrevocable.'[8] It is a natural human instinct to look for what we consider to be success in the work we put our hands to, but God's measure of success is different. He calls His servants to be faithful to the ministry into which He calls them. That sometimes means success in the eyes of people and sometimes not – it is God who gives the increase.[9] Someone once said, 'The burden that remains, that is from the Lord.' In God's divine economy many of His most valuable servants and the service they engage in are known to only a few people or sometimes even to none at all. The important thing to remember is that He sees everything and not even giving a glass of water to a child will go without reward.[10]

When Dave and Hilly first responded to the slip of paper which they had literally drawn out of a hat, which had Cornel's name and address on it, they did so out of a heart of Christian love and kindness. Some might even describe it as an altruistic urge, because thousands of people from the Western countries wanted to help people in Central and Eastern Europe after the fall of communism. Not all of them were Christians, but many were. Initially Dave and Hilly sent a letter with a parcel containing basic food supplies. Some weeks later they received a letter back from Cornel because he had taught himself English. So began a friendship through sending and receiving letters. As they did this, they couldn't

---

[8] Romans 11:29
[9] See 1 Corinthians 3:6
[10] See Matthew 10:42

know at that time that this was the beginning of a long-term ministry which God was calling them to. It was not their only ministry. Among other things they have consistently supported 'Prayer for Israel' and prayed for the peace of Jerusalem as the scripture tells us to.[11] Dave and Hilly's love and support for a severely disabled Christian, living in a small village 1,500 miles away, was indeed a calling from God and 'a calling that remains'. It demonstrates God's great heart of love and compassion expressed through His followers.

In those early years of their ministry to Cornel, communications were difficult. He didn't have a phone and their letters usually took about a month to reach their destination. Sometimes they tried sending small amounts of money in the letters but soon discovered that it often disappeared in transit! Things improved dramatically when Dave and Hilly obtained an Amstrad email phone (first introduced in 2000) which, as its name implies, combined email and a phone. People now smile at the thought of this obsolete electronic dinosaur, but it was a revolution in communications at the time. Later this was overtaken by computer-based email and then by Skype, both of which have been put to good use in their regular communications with Cornel. While Cornel was on his second visit to stay with Dave and Hilly, the vicar of the local St. Cuthbert's Church of England in Castle Vale was upgrading his own computer (he was an early computer enthusiast) and gave the motherboard from his old one to Cornel. He was able to take this back to Romania on the plane, along with a variety of tools and other items he acquired during that visit, helped by the friendly crew of the Romanian airline, Tarom, on which he travelled. He quickly became very proficient in using computers.

Dave and Hilly's first trip to Romania was in September 1994, when they were both aged forty-four. It was four years after the first contact had been made with Cornel by the Open Doors tour group which included Tony and Pat Romano, and fifteen months after Cornel's hip surgery at the Royal Orthopaedic Hospital in Birmingham. At that time there was a direct flight from Manchester to Constanta. Dave and Hilly were not seasoned travellers at this stage; their only foreign travel had been to visit Israel, pursuing their interest and burden to pray for Israel. Cornel's brother Viorel picked them up from the airport in his Dacia car and they stayed in Cornel's home with his parents for two weeks. It was

---

[11] Psalm 122:6

a big culture shock for them to say the least. Cumpăna at that time – in common with most rural villages in Romania – was not very developed. Many of the local people were poor compared with Western Europe and it was not unusual to see children running around without shoes. There were some cars, but many locals still used horses and carts. For Dave and Hilly it felt like stepping back in time. They remember enjoying looking at the night sky after dark – there were no street lights and little other 'light pollution' to spoil the magnificent view of God's creation.

Their toilet was a 'pit latrine' in the garden and the floor of the house was compacted mud. Maria had remembered from the six weeks she had stayed with Dave and Hilly that they liked the traditional English dish of sausage and mash. In an attempt to make them feel at home she served up the same dish. The problem was that Romanian sausages were very different, and Dave – quite literally – couldn't stomach them. Before the meal ended, he excused himself and rushed down the garden to the toilet, past their ferocious dog, Leutu (meaning 'little lion'), who was tied up in the garden, and vomited everything back up! Leutu didn't normally let anyone run past; perhaps he was napping on the job. Getting to the toilet always involved getting past Leutu, so Dave soon made a deal with him by bribing him with biscuits and they became the best of friends, making the calls of nature less nerve-racking! That was their first meal in Romania, but after that they enjoyed the meals that Maria prepared and came to love Romanian cuisine. They were able to meet Cornel's relatives, including Viorel, his wife and their seven children. One of their children was named Cornel David – Cornel after his uncle and David after Dave, because the child was born soon after Viorel's first visit to Britain with Cornel to see Mr Sterling. They also visited the Pentecostal church in Cumpăna and enjoyed fellowship with the local members. Dave was invited to speak at the service and was able to share his testimony, with Cornel translating. It was a moving time. Both Dave and Hilly were touched by the 'foot-washing' ceremony at the end, in which they participated.

There is little doubt that they would have followed up their first visit with more visits over the following years, but God had another ministry for them, and this would require the same faithfulness which He knew they had, and indeed, which He had given to them. It would also require most of their attention and dominate their lives. In December 1996, and without any warning, there was a ten-year-old child knocking at their door. It was Mark (not his real name), the child of a relative, and he had a note in his hand, asking them to look after him for the time being. Unknown to them at the time, his mother was hiding nearby to see if they would let him into their house – which of course they did. She promptly rushed away to an unknown destination.

Mark's parents were alcoholics who moved to different addresses fairly frequently and led a chaotic life. Dave and Hilly had two choices. Either they could hand Mark over to social services or make arrangements to officially foster him. Mark's young life had witnessed chaos, drunkenness and violence. It turned out that he and his mother had actually slept rough just prior to her abandoning him at Dave and Hilly's house and he was very glad to find himself in a 'normal' and peaceful home. So the decision was made that he should stay – a commitment that lasted for the next seven years!

Given his background, it is not surprising that in spite of Dave and Hilly's best efforts and the love that they constantly showed him, Mark soon began to make their lives difficult in various ways. The friends he chose were not a good influence and some of his behaviour was challenging, but God gave them the grace to remain faithful to the ministry that He had given to them in caring for him. They had no children of their own and therefore no parenting experience. They relied on the love of God and common sense to cope with a difficult teenager. Without their love and perseverance, he may well have found himself getting into trouble with the police.

When Mark, of his own free will, finally left at the age of seventeen, he mischievously told his mates that Dave and Hilly had thrown him out. This then caused them a lot of problems and stress. The mates decided that they should take revenge on Dave and Hilly on his behalf. During one eventful night (which happened to be the night before Dave and Hilly were due to go on holiday) they vandalised the front lawn of the house and poured the contents of the dustbin all over it. They daubed white gloss paint over the front door of the house and over the front windscreen of the car. Last of all they moved some metal pipes from a nearby building site and dumped them in the garden before running off. But God watches over his children in wonderful ways. It just so happened that Hilly needed to visit the bathroom at the front of the house during the night and heard the sound of one of those metal pipes. She went to look through a bedroom window just in time to see the fleeing lads. Through the darkness she could make out some of the mess on the lawn and woke

Dave up. Consequently, they went down and discovered the gloss paint before it had time to dry.

After a busy night of clearing it up they were able to drive off in the car next morning for the much-needed holiday. Around that time there were also a couple of broken windows and a failed attempt to burn down their front garden fence. Dave found all this particularly stressful. He believes that at the worst of these times he was close to a nervous breakdown. It is easy to quote scripture with hindsight, but God makes a promise in 1 Corinthians 10:13 that He will never allow His children to be tested more than they are able to bear. In fact, the testing only strengthens Christians in their faith and is in itself a mark of God's own trust in the work that He is doing in that Christian's life.

It was only about nine months before Dave and Hilly had taken Mark into their home that Cornel had married Cati, and in the summer of that year they both came to stay with Dave and Hilly for a couple of weeks. It was Cati's first time flying and travelling out of Romania and, although they didn't know it at the time, it was the last time the friends could be together for some years.

Although Dave and Hilly were unable to visit Romania while they were fostering Mark, they kept up their correspondence and support for Cornel and Cati. Eventually, nine years after their first visit to Cumpăna, they were at last able to go again. It was in the summer of 2005, and by then, Cami was a bright and pretty eight-year-old and they were delighted to meet her for the first time. This visit was followed by two more. 2009 was their first opportunity to meet Cornel and Cati's second daughter, Hilary Gabriela, the one named after Hilly, who was then about fifteen months old. By 2015, on their last visit to date, little Hilly had grown into a lively seven-year-old and Cami was a beautiful young woman aged eighteen.

———————

The story of Cornel and Cati would not be complete without looking at Dave's background in a little more detail, partly because of the long, crucial, friendship Dave and Hilly have had with Cornel (and now his family), but also to show the grace of God extended to Dave which has made him the person he is today. Jesus taught that those who are forgiven much love much. Dave's story is a good illustration of this.

Dave was born in Winson Green, Birmingham in 1950 – his parents' first child. They lived in one of the old back-to-back houses, long since condemned and demolished. When Dave was just four years old, his father died. By then he had two younger brothers, so his mum had her hands full. A few years later she married a man who turned out to be an abusive and violent alcoholic. He had two daughters from a previous marriage who also moved into the small family home.

By the time Dave was about eleven, another boy was born and they were all living in a two-bedroom flat! There was very little money and they were often in fear of their violent father/stepfather. Dave remembers them all hiding one night in the coal shed, which was outside, when he was due home from the pub late in the evening. There were other times when mum and the children all took cover in one of the bedrooms, with the outside handle removed, preventing entry.

By the time Dave was thirteen his mum was pregnant again. She must have been at her wits' end and tragically she took her own life. Within hours, Dave and his two brothers, together with their younger brother who was just a toddler, found themselves in an orphanage. The next day their little brother was taken from them, despite their protests, and the three of them were placed in a children's home in the Handsworth district of Birmingham. They lived in this place for about two years. Despite the terrible trauma that they had gone through, they actually found some stability in the care of the lovely couple who ran the home and have some good memories of that time. Sadly, it didn't last very long. They were moved into a foster home and it was not a happy placement.

As soon as Dave was able to leave school at sixteen, he chose to do 'live-in' farm work and was glad to leave the foster home. During his later teens, having no parents or family to turn to for love, support or guidance, he was attracted to the 1960s hippie movement. This inevitably drew him into taking drugs. It was a way of trying to escape the traumas and chaos of his early years. His behaviour deteriorated during those years and he was soon jobless and homeless. This went on for a couple of years, during which time he found himelf begging on the streets, not knowing where his next meal would come from. He also rummaged through bins and slept anywhere he could. Occasionally, friends he had made accommodated him for a night or two, but mostly it meant sleeping in shop doorways, on garage roofs and in derelict buildings etc.

From time to time he crossed paths with his younger brother whose life had followed a similar path. But on one particular occasion he told

Dave that his life had changed for the better because he had come to know Jesus as his saviour. He had recognised what a sinful person he was, and that he needed forgiveness and Jesus was the only way to real life. Dave was rather cynical at first and had doubts about the reality of his brother's experience. Each time he saw his brother after that, he made a point of watching to see if his life had really changed. After a period of about twelve months Dave could see that his brother's life really was different and had a direction and purpose which his own life lacked. Dave began to take the claims of Jesus more seriously.

He remembers one evening looking upwards and saying, "If you are the God my brother says you are, prove it. I will stop taking the drugs if you will deal with the difficulties of withdrawal." He stopped the drugs and waited to see what would happen – and he experienced no withdrawal problems. Jesus was real! Dave told God he was sorry for all the wrongdoings of the past and made a decision to follow Him. His life was totally changed. Sometime later he met and married Hilly, who was already a Christian, and a real blessing to him. Life still had various ups and downs, but because his life was now anchored in Christ, he was able to survive other storms that came his way.

For some time he still struggled with the after-effects of his traumatic early years. He was understandably fearful and anxious and frequently suffered very severe panic attacks. This continued for fifteen years. In desperation he went to an evening church meeting in response to an invitation to receive prayer. At the end of the meeting he responded to the invitation and went forward, but before anyone could pray for him, he cried out, "Jesus, have mercy on me." At that point he found himself on the floor, experiencing a warm tingling sensation and a tremendous sense of peace in his being. Having no idea how long he lay there, he eventually stood up and knew instantly that he had been set free from the panic attacks. Many years have passed and he has never experienced one since. Now in his late sixties he can honestly say that the best decision he ever made in his life was to follow Jesus. It was true then, and it is still just as true today.

Altruism: Good or Bad?

Most people would say that it is a good thing. Many people in places like Romania, Bulgaria and Ukraine were helped in the early days after the fall of communism in those countries. The same might be said of the many thousands of people who sponsor children in Africa and other relatively poor parts of this world. The thing that is sometimes missing from the donors is research, wisdom and cultural knowledge. Most church pastors in sub-Saharan Africa say that putting orphaned children into Western-financed institutions is not a good idea. This is because they become separated from their culture and don't learn the skills needed for their future life, and this creates a 'dependency culture'. To balance this 'from the West to the rest' mentality, we should remember that one man's 'dependency culture' is another man's answer to prayer!

John Miles tried to concentrate on helping the churches in Romania in the first few years after the revolution and he observed the astonishing amount of 'aid' being transported by ordinary members of the public and churches. About eighteen months after Romania's revolution, he had a phone call from one of the new charities that had been recently set up as part of sincere efforts to help in former communist countries. He was asked if he would like the contents of a thirty-eight-tonne truck, full of aid. It would not cost him a penny, he just needed to supply the address and it would be delivered there. He said he would ask the contacts he had in the Romanian churches to see if they wanted this valuable aid. To his surprise, every one of the half dozen pastors he asked said no. The aid was too much trouble, it caused arguments between the recipients, and anyway, they were too busy coping with their expanded post-revolution pastoral ministry to spend their days distributing aid and settling disputes over it.

Cornel's first two visits to England had been for his medical treatment and his third was the one shortly after his marriage to Cati. There was one more visit, accompanied by both Cati and Cami (then aged ten), when again they stayed with Dave and Hilly for two weeks. This was in July 2007, and Dave and Hilly fondly remember the great fun they had touring charity shops. The Lemnariu family were delighted and surprised at the amazing array of items on offer at very low prices. But that visit was different from the others in one very important aspect, and this would change everything!

CHAPTER ELEVEN

From Romania With Love

THE EVENT THAT CHANGED EVERYTHING IN ROMANIA could be described as 'another revolution', such was its effect on the people, the government, and most of all, on the country's economy. On 1st January 2007, Romania and Bulgaria joined the European Union (EU). The actual accession of Romania and Bulgaria had been held back for three years. The ten countries which actually joined in 2004 were Cyprus, Czech Republic, Estonia, Hungary, Latvia, Lithuania, Malta, Poland, Slovak Republic and Slovenia. Romania had first applied to join in June 1995 and the following twelve years were a period of making reforms and adjustments to their institutions and legal system, in a sincere attempt to meet the EU's requirements for joining. The Ceauşescu regime had borrowed heavily during the 1970s, and by 1982 the debt had reached a point where he could borrow no more, reaching a colossal $13 billion. The regime imposed severe austerity measures, banning almost all imports. This resulted in the population suffering greatly from food and fuel shortages. Ceauşescu even used some of Romania's limited supply of food to pay for oil imports. By 1989 the debt was mostly paid off but the angry reaction of the population who had suffered so much deprivation helped pave the way for the 1989 revolution.

The most significant change that Romania's accession had was that Romanians could now travel freely, without visas, to other EU countries – and many of them did. Some Western countries feared mass migration from Romania and Bulgaria, the two poorest countries in the bloc (apart perhaps from Albania), so transitional controls were imposed. These allowed visits but permanent settlement with rights to employment and a range of benefits were not available to migrants for their first seven years. These controls were lifted in 2014 when Greece took over the six-month rotating presidency of the EU.

For many migrants the intention was to work for some years, learn the language, make some money and then return home in a better financial position. Many Romanians did this, but others decided to stay in the countries to which they had migrated. Britain is one of the most popular destinations for Romanians but many also went to other European countries, especially Italy and Spain, where there are similarities between their Latin languages. Austria was also popular because of the close geographical proximity, making it easier to drive to and from Romania. The British government's 'Office of National Statistics' revealed that the number of Romanian nationals estimated to be living in the UK in 2017 was 411,000, a 25% increase since 2016 and the biggest increase recorded for people from any country, contributing to a UK population that reached a new high of 66,000,000, one of the most densely populated countries in the world.

Cornel's brother Viorel was married to Elena (known as Lenuta) and they had seven children, five boys and two girls. This family also lived in Cumpăna and often helped Cornel whenever he needed it. The two girls were the oldest and the second of the boys to arrive was named Viorel after his father and usually referred to as Vio.

Ana grew up in Medgidia (about forty-four kilometres from Cumpăna) and was one of ten siblings. She attended the main Pentecostal church in Medgidia with her family. Occasionally, the church in Medgidia would send their youth group to the church in Constanta for joint meetings and events. In this way Vio met Ana and they began to see each other at youth meetings. Many of the youth in Cumpăna and Medgidia often visited the larger church in Constanta because they had a very good youth programme which included free lessons on musical instruments. The young couple began to see more of each other, fell in love and decided to marry. Vio is intelligent, enterprising and hard-working. When it comes to the Romanian culture which regards any problem as 'no problem', Vio is an outstanding example.

While they were at university, Vio began to think about their future together. They were fairly poor and Vio could not see how their fortunes could change much in the near future. He knew that many Romanians were travelling to other EU countries to find better jobs, save money and then return home with enhanced financial prospects. He decided that he would do the same. He dropped out of university and worked hard at two jobs for six months to save enough money to travel to the UK. His uncle Cornel had told him how things were in England and he decided that this was the place he should go. His plan was to find a job for six months, save as much as he could and then return home to marry Ana, who was still at university training to be a teacher.

Vio signed up with an agency that helped Romanians find work in the UK and promised them that they could get the coveted 'Yellow Card' which was the nickname for the official work permit. They promised all this in exchange for £1,000, which needed to be paid before departure to the UK and was the equivalent to six months' pay of Vio's salary in Romania. Vio had never travelled outside Romania before; this was a journey into the unknown for him. He travelled by coach and arrived in the UK in May 2011, aged twenty-one. The job that the agency had arranged for him turned out to be in a car wash, which many young Romanian men were doing as their first job in the UK. Vio's job was in Bedford near London and his boss was an Albanian.

The accommodation provided was a small house that his boss rented to house his workers and which was shared by thirteen of them. He worked hard for ten hours a day for the first three days and was so depressed that he was ready to give up. He phoned his old boss back in Romania, who was also a Christian, and he really wanted Vio to come back. Vio just wasn't sure what he should do, but as he prayed about it, he concluded that God had not brought him to England just for three days. He carried on doing his best and working hard. His Christian background had taught him that whatever job he did, he should do it heartily as unto the Lord.[12]

After three weeks Vio' boss was so impressed with him that he asked him, "Have you got any more like you?"

Vio said, "Yes, my brother Marius." Marius is one year older than Vio and he arrived in July 2011.

In August his boss asked him the same question again and his reply was, "Yes, my brother Lucian."

Lucian (who was twenty years old) arrived in the UK in September 2011.

---

[12] See Colossians 3:23-24

Vio was becoming the trailblazer for what was becoming a family migration, and so it proved, as eventually over the next five years all six siblings settled in the UK. Vio and his brothers were demonstrating a well-known fact that migrants from Central or Eastern European and Baltic countries are prepared to come to the UK, work hard and long hours for a minimum rate of pay, and in jobs that British people are often reluctant to do. Consequently, they are in demand from employers. Many, including Vio, saw this as a first step to better things ahead.

Vio was determined not to stay and work in the UK illegally. For him it was essential to have the correct paperwork. After two months he challenged his boss about the Yellow Card that the agency had promised as part of their deal. The boss smiled and said, "Who told you that?" He informed Vio that he was sorry but he didn't do that. It was obvious that Vio and his brothers were going to have to provide their paperwork themselves. They worked hard for the next five months and saved enough money to pay for the Yellow Card. To avoid a long wait and uncertainty, he again used an agency, which meant that he and Marius had an appointment at the immigration office in Croydon in south London. It also meant that they were able to obtain the work permit with a single visit there. The cost for the service and the Yellow Card was £3,000 each! Then, once they had the work permit, they could get a National Insurance number. This meant that six months after Vio arrived, he and Marius were now legally working in the UK.

Having obtained their Yellow Cards and National Insurance numbers, the way was open for Vio and Marius to register with a proper employment agency – which they did. Thousands of new migrants from the EU are offered jobs in hotels and restaurants. Again, the reason is their willingness to work long hours at or near to the minimum wage. They soon received a phone call from the agency, and they were offered a job in the Lake District working in a restaurant. Their job was at the Village Inn in Bowness-on-Windermere, a popular restaurant just one hundred metres from the famous lake – a beautiful location in which to work. Lucian stayed at the car wash and was soon joined by other relatives.

They arrived in Windermere on 2nd October 2011. They were sent by the agency to fill two posts: one as a waiter and the other as a kitchen porter. The problem was that neither of them had enough English to be a waiter. There was not enough work in the kitchen for the two of them long-term, which meant that they had a choice to make: one of them had to leave. Vio said it was best for him to leave because he had a little more English than Marius and would be better able to find other work. He decided to go to London where he was fairly sure he could find work, especially as he was now a fully legal worker. By Easter the following year, another job became available in the restaurant and the boss asked Marius if he knew of anyone to fill it. He recommended Lucian[13], who then joined his brother working at the Village Inn. It was much better than the carwash or labouring jobs in London.

Vio left for London by train on 30th October. He arrived at Euston Station at 1.00 pm and intended to stay in the station until the next morning and then go out looking for work. What he didn't know was that Euston station closed at 1.00 a.m. and everyone still in the station had to vacate. This was broadcast over the station's public address system. He felt a little panicky because he had nowhere to go and there were some unsavoury-looking characters hanging around outside the station. He had arrived in London full of self-confidence that he would soon find a job and somewhere to stay. Of course, it was more complicated than that. You can't get a legitimate job without a home address, which he didn't have, and he knew no one in London.

As he sat there on a bench in the station, he began to think. He realised that he had left God out of his thinking and was trying to achieve things in his own strength. He prayed and told God that he was sorry for this and wanted to trust Him, and not in his own abilities. Now God stepped in and began to show Vio how much he could rely on God to look after him. After he prayed, and shortly before the station closed, a man named Gerard came and sat next to him and began reading a Bible. Then he began to speak with Vio, who didn't really want to speak to anyone and didn't know much English anyway. The man was friendly and offered him a place to stay that night at his home. The fact that he was reading a Bible helped Vio to decide to go with him.

Gerard took him home and the next day gave him a lift to the station and some money for the train fare to Croydon, where he had an appointment later that day at the immigration office. He made it to the appointment alright, but he still had nowhere to stay that night. One of Vio's sisters in Romania heard about his situation and began circulating news of his predicament to other families that she knew had relatives in London. He was contacted by phone and was offered accommodation

---

[13] Lucian was another brother who was still working in a car wash.

for a week at a time with a Romanian family and subsequently by two single Romanian ladies living in London who knew his family. He couldn't stay in his accommodation during the day, so he just went from one place to another looking for a job.

By the end of the first week, he had not found one and was feeling very depressed. Then God stepped in again in an amazing way. He was walking across the bridge over the rail lines in Kenton Road, near Kenton Station, head down, thinking he must leave the next day; then a young woman passed him walking in the opposite direction. She stopped and called his name. He wondered who this person could be who knew his name, and then he recognised her. It was a girl he had grown up with, who had lived in Constanta, and their mothers were good friends. Her name was Alina and she lived nearby. She asked him, "What are you doing here, Vio?" He told his story and she replied, "You must come and stay with us!" She and her husband had recently married and only had a one-bedroom flat, so it wasn't a suitable place for him to stay long-term – but it met his immediate need. This meeting was such an extreme coincidence, only God could have arranged it! Later, her brother who was already living in London, whom Vio also knew, came and suggested he stay with him for two weeks. Once again, Vio could see that God was looking after him.

By now it was January 2012. He found a job as a labourer on a building site with a company named Windhurst, and the pay was very good. His boss was another Romanian and everyone worked hard in spite of the winter conditions. It was a proper company that took care of his tax and National Insurance payments in the normal way, even though their workers were mostly classed as self-employed.

Another family in the church in Romania heard about his need of accommodation. They had a relative who worked in London, and he offered to share his room with Vio on a longer-term basis. He was now working, had a work permit, paid tax, National Insurance, and had a home address. He was fully legal and fairly settled, just nine months after arriving in the UK.

After six months in this job he was asked to help the foreman in charge of the group of Romanian workers on the site (who didn't speak much English) with his communications. Vio was now speaking better English than the others he was adept at using his Romanian book on how to learn English, and he also attended college to learn English in the evenings. By this time, he had decided that he wanted to stay long-term in England, but he was appalled at the poor and overcrowded conditions that most ex-pat Romanians lived in. This was due to the high cost of accommodation in London, and Vio didn't want to stay there. He looked at the map of Britain and saw that Birmingham was a large city, probably with jobs available for people who were not fussy about what work they did. While he was working on the Windhurst building site, he noticed that there were often minibuses that daily carried handicapped people to their places of work or sheltered employment, then home again. The idea of working as a driver for this kind of transport really appealed to him. He asked God if it would be possible for him to have this kind of job. It was more than a random idea; he really felt that he wanted to do that kind of work.

Now that Vio had decided that he wanted to live in the UK, Ana also wanted to plan for their future together. If she completed her teacher training at university, would this qualification be recognised in the UK? She made enquiries and found out that it would not be accepted and so there was no point in completing the course. In the longer term, she still wanted to be a teacher, but this would mean training locally. This led to the decision for her to apply for jobs in the UK too. After two weeks she was offered a job as an au pair in Littleover, near Derby, and she arrived in February 2012. This made sense because Ana could also earn a salary in England before their upcoming wedding.

They now needed to decide where in Britain they would live after their wedding. They knew about Dave and Hilly from Cornel, and so made contact asking if they could visit to ask for their advice. They had a good time with Dave and Hilly and wondered if Birmingham was the place they should be aiming for. They made a few enquiries about the cost of renting a home there and compared the costs with those in London. At this stage they were also busy with arranging their wedding in Constanta so the enquiry for a home in Birmingham was not too serious; it was just research. Dave and Hilly thought and prayed about Vio and Ana's situation and eventually invited them to come and stay with them after their wedding, while they found work and a place to stay.

Vio and Ana now had a plan for the future. Their first step was to return to Romania for their wedding which was on 29th July 2012 in the main Pentecostal church in Constanta. They remained in Romania for a further six months. During that time Vio undertook training to gain driving licences for Public Service Vehicles (PSV) and both categories of Heavy Goods Vehicles (HGV). This training in the UK costs thousands of pounds, but a fraction of that in Romania. With Romania now in the EU, the licences were valid in the UK.

So it was that they came to the UK on 13th January 2013 and were accommodated with Dave and Hilly in Castle Vale for the next five months. During this period Vio began applying for jobs. Dave and Hilly helped the couple face the reality that if they didn't find a job, they would have to consider returning to Romania. Ana shed tears at this thought because they believed that God had brought them to where they were.

Vio went for a walk along the nearby Birmingham to Fazeley canal and cried out to God in desperation. Before he had finished praying, his mobile phone rang. It was a staff agency based in the nearby town of Tamworth that he had registered with, and they asked him to go for an interview.

To his amazement, the job was for the position of a minibus driver for handicapped people! They asked him why he wanted this kind of job and he explained that he had grown up living near his uncle Cornel in Cumpăna and had often helped him, so he had developed an affinity for handicapped people. They offered him the job, which was in Birmingham, and it was at a day centre in the district of Moseley in the south of the city. He started work there on 13th February and really enjoyed the work, impressing everyone with his enthusiasm and dedication. The only problem was that it wasn't a permanent job; he was only on a temporary contract. After six months his manager heard that there was a permanent position as a driver at a day centre in the district of Erdington, which is adjacent to Castle Vale. He advised Vio to apply for it because he realised that it would be better for Vio and Ana, who wanted to buy a house and start a family. His good performance and work ethic in Moseley ensured a good reference from his manager and his application was successful.

After six months in the Erdington job, his former manager in Moseley phoned him and asked him to return to Moseley because there was now a permanent position available for him there. Vio was very pleased to be asked to go back even though it was further to travel. The Erdington centre was small and under threat of closure.

The Moseley centre was purpose-built and the largest in the city. The city council did not control the land on which it was built and therefore could never sell it. The land was formerly part of the Cadbury family (famous for their chocolate) estate and was donated to the city under conditions that it was not sold for other purposes. Uffculme House, which is a grade two listed building, is also nearby and was the home of Richard Cadbury and his family from 1890 to 1906. A further attraction for Vio was that the centre had a garden project and he loved helping with that when he wasn't out driving.

On 31st May 2013, Vio and Ana moved from Dave and Hilly's house to a rented flat in Erdington. Their lovely daughter Rebecca was born in February 2014. By saving as much money as they could, they eventually had enough for a ten percent deposit on a house and purchased one on 27th February 2014. It is a modern three-bedroom terraced house, in – of all places – Castle Vale! Then to add blessing upon blessing from God, their house is just a few minutes' walk from the home of their good friends Dave and Hilly. At the time of writing this, Vio is still working at the Moseley day centre and loves the job. His employers love him because of his enthusiasm and willingness to do anything asked of him whether it is in his job description or not. Vio knows that he has a lot to thank God for, not least his lovely family.

CHAPTER TWELVE

Some Dreams Come True

THE LIFE OF THE LEMNARIU FAMILY NOW SETTLED INTO A pattern of trying to survive as best they could. Cornel's condition needed regular but expensive medication. New treatment was now available in Romania that could halt the otherwise relentless progress of the ankylosing spondylitis and ease the pain. This is a medication called Enbrel, which is the trade name for etanercept, a biopharmaceutical that treats various forms of rheumatoid arthritis as well as ankylosing spondylitis. Although it became available in Romania, it was often very difficult to find. Cornel and Cati frequently had to travel far and wide, going to every pharmacy in Constanta searching for the medication – and sometimes they just didn't find it. Cornel could be without it for several months until they found some again. Without the medication Cornel's pain increased and the erosion of his joint mobility continued.

Cornel still needed regular blood tests and steroid medication. There was a little help from the Romanian health service, but they had to cover the bulk of the costs themselves. Even the prescriptions for the medication required bribes to be given to the doctors before they would write them. At first, they travelled around in the yellow Dacia 1300 that Cornel had bought from his brother Viorel when he went to work in Germany. Their second car was a Dacia Break, which was an improvement on the old yellow Dacia. Then in 2009 they were able to buy a Dacia Logan which was newer and more reliable.

The cost of everything was their greatest problem. Cornel couldn't do a regular job, and his photography business had dwindled as people began buying smartphones and taking their own digital photographs. Cati couldn't do a regular job because she was caring for Cornel and their two daughters. Just searching for Cornel's medication and transporting him to his various appointments made working the fixed hours that a regular job required impossible. She even went as far as making the traditional building blocks out of yellow mud and selling them. It was hard work but it brought in some income to help with family finances. Some of their food came from their garden and the domestic animals and chickens that they reared. All these things helped but it was not enough. Once again, it was God's provision with financial help from friends in Britain that made life manageable.

Cornel's first computer, given to him by John Miles through his friends in the UK, was very basic compared with later models; but for Cornel it was an important introduction into the world of computing. The development of computers was very rapid and Cornel did well in keeping up with it. He was fascinated by computers and loved working on them. He could never afford to splash out on the more expensive new models, but this turned out to be an advantage. He bought used models and when he took them for repair, he watched carefully as they were worked on. He was soon able to do repairs not only for himself, but for other people. He began to build his own more powerful computers. He realised that his limited mobility was no handicap at all once he was sat in front of a screen. He learned how to copy old video cassettes onto the computer, edit them and then transpose them onto DVDs. Once he had access to the Internet, he entered the digital world where anything that he needed to know or wanted to learn was available via search engines such as Google. On one of his later computers he began to learn video editing. In the longer term, he saw this as a possible way for him to earn a living.

Between May 2011, when Vio was the first of Cornel's nephews to move to the UK, and December 2015, all five of Cornel's nephews and one of his two nieces – all children of Viorel and Lenuta – arrived to live in the UK. The thought that Cornel and Cati might be able to do the same often entered their thoughts and conversation. The obstacles to the idea were formidable. The nephews were young and eager to work and contribute to their new country. They too wanted to move, but just couldn't see how it would be possible. But they had a history of seeing God overcome obstacles for them and so they kept up hope and an open mind. They had both been to the UK and knew they could be happy living there.

Added to this was the pressing need for Cornel to access the right medication consistently and have his condition cared for in a much more effective way. After about two years on the effective biological medication, it was decided that he should no longer have this treatment because it was considered to be "ineffective" in his case. It was not Cornel's consultant that decided this; she was mystified because she knew it was helping her patient a lot. Under the health system in Romania at that time, these decisions were taken by a committee of doctors in Bucharest without even seeing the patient. We can only guess as to their reasoning. It may have been the cost of the treatment which could be needed for many years to come, even though the state only paid towards the cost and the patient had to find the rest. Britain has its own system for evaluating treatments. It is referred to by its abbreviation 'NICE' (The National Institute for Health and Care Excellence). Their decisions are sometimes a controversial balance between cost and benefit to the patient group in need of the treatment. Many other countries have their own equivalent system.

Their long-time wish to move to the UK seemed impossible until other family members had emigrated. This raised the question, would they have enough help if they moved? The political and immigration barriers had been removed when Romania joined the EU, and further restrictions had been removed in 2014, but the financial challenges remained formidable. Where would they live? They needed wheelchair access for Cornel, which meant ground floor accommodation without steps to gain entry.

Cati had half-seriously asked Vio, who by now had lived in England for five years, if he would like them to also come and live in UK. He said – with the typical Romanian response to obstacles – "Yes, you can come anytime." It was going to be 'no problem'. Cornel and Cati held this thought and ambition in the back of their minds during those years. Then the thought was propelled to the forefront of their minds when they began to hear about Brexit! Prime Minister David Cameron and most of the British establishment were convinced that the country would accept the PM's strong recommendation and vote to stay in the EU. It was revealed as one of the greatest miscalculations in British political history when, on 23rd June 2016, a majority of Britain's citizens (17.4 million) on a high turnout voted to leave.

In the early days after the referendum, there arose the question of the rights of previous migrants to the UK, and UK citizens living in the EU. 3.8 million EU citizens lived in the UK (2018 figure) and 1.3 million UK citizens lived in EU countries (2017 figure). Apart from the question of rights for existing migrants, what would be the position of those wanting to move but were still thinking about it or planning it? It was now imperative for anyone planning to come to the UK to begin to make up their minds and work out the feasibility for them to move while the door was still open. Governments throughout the EU, including Britain, were quick to assure people that existing rights would be preserved and protected. For former Iron Curtain countries such as Romania, Bulgaria, Poland and Hungary, the assurances of governments were not enough to remove anxiety and a growing sense of urgency. They had, after all, grown up in countries where assurances from governments were not to be taken seriously at all!

Cornel and Cati didn't want to wait for the result of any referendum. They had long ago decided they would like to live in the UK. Cati often asked Cornel, "When are we going?" Many of Cornel's relatives had already moved to the UK under the freedom of movement provisions of the Treaty of Rome. Life was becoming much more difficult for Cornel once the only medication that helped him had been stopped, and he was again in a lot of pain. He decided it was now or never. Cornel made a Skype call to his nephew Vio in February 2016 and expressed their wish to move and to do so soon. He asked him if there was a possibility of accommodation for them. Vio's reply was predictable: "No problem." Two of his brothers who had come to Britain had rented a flat in Nuneaton, a medium-sized town in the Shire County of Warwickshire, with a population of 92,000. His two brothers would move to live with other brothers temporarily and they could use the flat.

A final decision had to be made. On April 1st, 2016, Cornel asked Cati and Cami if they really wanted to move to Britain. Cati's reply was, "Yes, you have asked me this many times."

Cornel said, "Okay we will go; I have already bought the tickets online."

It was April 1st and the thought crossed Cati's mind that this might be an April fools' joke that Cornel was playing. Romania has the same April 1st tradition as Britain does (along with nine other countries). Her reaction was, "I don't believe you."

Cornel assured her that he was serious and they could actually go. Once Vio said that he could organise a place for them to live in Nuneaton, this had been the deciding factor.

They didn't even have passports at the time and so they had to move quickly to make all the arrangements. Dave and Hilly were amazed when they heard that they were coming. Throughout their long friendship with

Cornel and Cati, they never thought that this would be possible, and they were thrilled at the unexpected news.

The moving date was set for 18th April 2016. Cornel was aged fifty-one, Cati was forty-one, Cami was a spectacular beauty at nineteen and (little) Hilly was a bright eight-year-old. They flew from Constanta to Luton on the Hungarian budget airline Wizzair. Vio met them at the airport and, naturally, Dave and Hilly were also there, eager to greet them.

Cati's mother had already moved to live with two of her daughters and a son in Austria. Cati's father had also gone with Maria to Austria, but he didn't like it there and soon returned to Cumpăna; he died shortly afterwards. In 2018 Maria returned to Cumpăna but she was very ill with heart problems. Cornel and Cati kept their house and their car in Cumpăna as a sort of insurance policy. If things went wrong, they could always go back there as a last resort.

Once they had settled in Nuneaton, near the end of April, they went to register with the local GP surgery, but were not accepted because they didn't yet have a National Insurance number. Then they tried a second GP surgery and were accepted because they had valid EU passports and this entitled them to apply for National Insurance numbers. The nurse in the practice asked what medications Cornel was using. She was not able to supply everything he needed because some could only be prescribed by a specialist. The GP then referred him to the local George Eliot hospital where his consultant was Dr Al Sweedan. At his first appointment in August 2016 there were lots of tests to determine his condition and the medication he needed. Then, once the results were in, his consultant explained that there were several options for his situation and asked him which one he wished to go ahead with.

Cornel chose the Enbrel which he knew was effective for him. He now administers this with a self-injection 'pen'. The supplies are delivered to his home every other month in a cool box and they are stored in his fridge. It took only about three months from when they left Romania that Cornel began to receive the biological medication that he desperately needed, and he didn't need to pay or search for it. Once again, God had stepped in and provided for him in a wonderful way.

About a month after they arrived in Nuneaton, they purchased a used car for Cati to be able to travel to the part-time job she had found at the Swan Inn, where she worked in the kitchen washing up, preparing the desserts and generally helping the chef. Cati is a very good cook and sometimes bakes lovely cakes to order for special occasions. After nine months she was made redundant from this job and was unemployed for two months before finding another job at the Longshoot Hotel, also working in the kitchen of this very busy hotel. When Cornel was still in Romania, he heard about the Motability charity in the UK, but when they first arrived, they could not immediately access the scheme. Once Cornel's disability had been assessed, he was eligible to apply.

On 9th August he applied for the government's Personal Independence Payment (PIP) which had replaced the Disability Living Allowance. This was awarded to Cornel in December 2016. The payment allows disabled people and their families to use the money to lease a new car under the Motability scheme. Their monthly payment includes tax and insurance for the car. The scheme has more than 650,000 customers in the UK. It was a crucial benefit for Cornel and his family, giving them access to suitable and reliable transport with a boot large enough for his wheelchair. Cati's driving licence was valid in the UK and she quickly adapted to driving on the other side of the road. After a few months, they were able to rent a house in Nuneaton that was suitable for wheelchair access.

Their younger daughter Hilly was eight years old and didn't speak much English, so she didn't begin school immediately. Having arrived in April, she didn't start at school until September. She studied English at home with the aid of videos and then she began school at the local Nursery Hill Primary School. At the end of that year (July 2017) she was still catching up with the others of her age. After a further year she had made spectacular progress and was awarded the school's 'Golden plate' as their 'pupil of the year'. She had learnt English, caught up with the rest of her class and finished the year in the top 20% – a wonderful achievement. Cami began studies at Coventry University, but the difficulty of commuting there on public transport from Nuneaton, and the costs, meant that she gave it up in favour of the same course studied from home. On 3rd June 2017, Cami married Marius (a Romanian friend who had lived in the UK for several years) at the Elim Pentecostal church in Nuneaton where the family regularly worshipped. They made a handsome couple.

Epilogue

TO ADEQUATELY APPRECIATE THE AMAZING JOURNEY THAT God has brought Cornel and Cati through, it is important to remember where and how it all began. Cornel was a handicapped person, living with his parents in a small village that hardly anyone had heard of, and in a country that, at that time, had a very poor view of handicapped people. His chances of finding help from Christians visiting from another country two thousand miles away were, humanly speaking, so remote that only God could have organised it. The coach party arriving on the right night because there wasn't a Christian meeting in Constanta, and Cornel turning up at the same meeting, one that he normally wouldn't be able to attend, again, only God could organise. The rest of the story is a series of interlocking jigsaw pieces which God put together.

Cornel has suffered an enormous amount of pain and inadequate medical treatment in his life. It is his unshakable faith in God that has sustained him throughout. His stubborn belief that God is good and watches over him is the one great demonstration of faith and trust to which God responds. His medical condition was left undiagnosed and mistreated until the age of eighteen. Once his condition was diagnosed correctly, he was informed that he would not live beyond the age of thirty. But at the age of fifty-one he arrived in the UK just three days short of his twentieth wedding anniversary, accompanied by his wife and two daughters. God has proved that when He steps into a person's life, normal rules simply do not apply. The medical treatment and medication that Cornel now receives are literally life-saving. Only God knows Cornel's eventual lifespan, but all Cornel needs to know is God; and that is the end of all such discussion.

Cati also suffered pain, astonishing cruelty and deprivation at the hands of uncaring parents and other relatives. At times in her teens, neighbours secretly even gave her shampoo because no one would buy it for her. Such was the level of neglect. She too possessed a stubborn faith in a Heavenly Father that loved her and had a plan for her life. It was one that she could only dream about. At an early age she learned to work hard, and this has been one of the themes of her life. Even though she now lives in Nuneaton, she cooks, cleans, helps Cornel, works part time and drives Cornel and herself to hospital appointments, shopping, church, and – best of all – trips to see family and friends; especially those local heroes Dave and Hilly.

Jesus said it is more blessed to give than receive,[14] and the givers of this world know that this is true. Giving and receiving is a two-way street; the blessing and reward for the givers and the helpers balance the joy and gratitude of the receivers. It is impossible to out-give God. As the great Apostle Paul put it, 'Thanks be to God for His indescribable gift!'[15] What greater gift could anyone receive than eternal life through the Lord Jesus Christ? To God be all the glory. Amen.

[14] See Acts 20:35
[15] 2 Corinthians 9:15

Similar Books from the Publisher

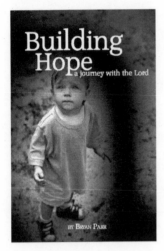

Building Hope
Bryan Parr
ISBN 978-1-907509-13-1

If you want to know what happens when someone past fifty, sitting at the back of his church, says to God, "Surely there's more than this!" then read this book. Bryan and Slyvia's willingness took them to Russia and Romania, among other places, and showed them that they could make a difference. Read... Be inspired... Go and do likewise.

Unjustified Joy
Leah-Maarit Jeffery
ISBN 978-1-78815-643-1

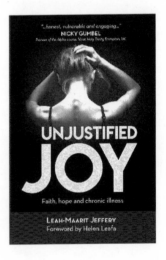

Leah had emigrated to Australia and gained citizenship, working as a graphic designer. However, when a mysterious condition developed, causing increasing main and decreased mobility, the doctors were puzzled as all test results came back negative. Eventually, Leah was flown back to her childhood home in the UK, where she was diagnosed with an aggressive form of the chronic disease ankylosing spondylitis. As a Christian, Leah found that the difficult years to follow would be the moulding, shaping and testing of her faith.

AVAILABLE FROM ALL GOOD BOOKSHOPS